the feminist seventies

edited by
helen graham • ann kaloski
ali neilson • emma robertson

RAW NERVE BOOKS

First published in 2003 by
Raw Nerve Books Limited
Centre for Women's Studies
University of York
York YO10 5DD
England
www.rawnervebooks.co.uk

The authors have asserted their moral right to be identified as the authors of this work under the Copyright, Designs and Patents Act, 1988.

British Library Cataloguing-in publication Data. A catalogue record for this book is available from the British Library.
ISBN: 0-9536585-5-4

Image design by Esperanza Miyake. Book and cover design by Hilary Kay Doran.

Printed and bound by York Publishing Services Limited,
64 Hallfield Road, Layerthorpe, York, YO31 7ZQ

The Feminist Seventies is part of an innovative linked publication: a free-to-access web book and a companion print book.

Helen Graham, Ann Kaloski, Ali Neilson, Emma Robertson (eds) *The Feminist Seventies* web book (June, 2003) ISBN: 0-9536585-4-6; <www.feminist-seventies.net/webbook.html>

contents

Dedication

To all women, then and now, who fight for a peaceful world.

Acknowledgements

As always with such a collaborative undertaking many people have helped to bring this book to fruition. In particular, we would like to thank:

- Participants at The Feminist Seventies Conference, University of York, April 2002, for making the day such a vibrant, thought-provoking and often surprising event. We hope this book is worthy of their effort and imagination, and serves to generate yet more inspiring and constructive feminist work.

- The rest of the conference coordinating group who were so resourceful and industrious – Joan Heggie, Anne Fairbank, Trev Broughton – as well as those who worked so tirelessly on the day and behind the scenes – Esperanza Miyake, Yvette Taylor, Janaki Jayawardena, Jo Woodiwiss, Esther Ho, Julia Nxumalo, Amanda Brooks, Noelia Diaz Vicedo, Julie Palmer, Amy Rootvik and Jean Wall. We would also like to remember Susan Pearson who was an integral part of the early conference discussions and who, sadly, died in March 2002.

- Contributors to both this book and its companion web book, for risk-taking and rigour in their writing, diligence during the editing process, and for generously entering into the radical publishing ethos of Raw Nerve.

- Esperanza Miyake for the witty and wonderful cover image, and Hilary Doran for her adroit combination of creativity and pragmatism in designing this book, and for her never-ending patience with us through all the formatting procedures.

- The veritable legion of advisory and proof readers who offered their time so freely and effectively: Tania Angeloff, Neil Armstrong, Trev Broughton, Carl Creswell, Sarah Hutton, Mike Kaloski-Naylor, Catriona Kennedy, Michele Learner, Linda Perriton, Elizabeth Seneviratne, Liz Sourbut, Michael Terwey, Merran Toerian and Louise Wannell.

- The Centre for Women's Studies and the Department of English, University of York, for their continued practical support and encouragement. <www.york.ac.uk>

- Bob Naylor and Joan Heggie for much appreciated help with the accounts.

- Dave Mercer, Cathi Poole, Duncan Beal, Caroline Hall, and all at York Publishing Services for continued efficiency and good humour. <www.yps-publishing.co.uk>

Due to the nature of WLM source materials, which are often found without named author or official publisher, we have been unable to obtain copyright for some quoted material. We hope, however, that we have used the women's words, cartoons and ideas in the spirit they were originally intended, and we would be very happy to include full details in subsequent editions: please contact Raw Nerve with any information.

Preface

I ♥ the 1970s.

Over the last few years, nostalgia has been sweeping the UK or, at least, BBC 2's Saturday night schedules. In the type of programmes which have 'I ♥' in the title, 'the seventies' is conjured up through bright images of Abba, purple flares over dangerously high platform shoes and by prompting childhood memories of space hoppers and Grange Hill. Those were the days, the audience sigh.

Of course, even today in a time of twenty-first century nostalgia 'the seventies' connotes much more than this. And for the purposes of this book, not least, 'women's liberation'. If 'I ♥1970s' boils down to flare-wearing Abba – what simple shorthand might apply to British women's liberation in the seventies? Dungarees perhaps? Burning bras? Placards? Consciousness raising? Cue the nostalgia programming guide to feminism: remember the flour bombs, the protests, the poetry readings . . .

I ♥ the *feminist* seventies?

Certainly the dangers of forgetting feminism's past has caused concern for a number of writers. Jill Radford, in her article 'History of Women's Liberation Movements in Britain: A Reflexive Personal History', attempts to 'look back at threads from our past, in order to re-view, re-vise, re-new, re-connect and where necessary reject them, to ensure that in plotting the voyage forward, we are at least informed by our history' (1994:41). By explaining the significance of the past to feminism's future, Radford argues that women who were there have a responsibility 'to reflect on our memories, to enable the next generation of feminists to build on our strengths and learn from our mistakes' (1995:40). The importance of experience is also a theme of Sheila

Rowbotham's work. Warning future feminism against needless repetition, Rowbotham suggests that 'by mining our memories we might save someone time in the future' (1989:299) and she evokes the image of the past as a map which lays open and makes visible the political landscape (eg 1979:54) offering us, she hopes, a 'sense of direction' (1989:301).

Forgetting is, however, the least of feminism's problems. It is when the seventies are remembered that the real problems start. Unlike viewers of its schedule-filler counterpart, remembering feminism in the seventies is by no means confined to a depressing Saturday night in – it has become an academic pursuit for any day of the week. As Jackie Stacey has suggested, the game of 'I remember', if not 'I ♥', 'seventies feminism' most often falls into two camps. On one side nostalgia rules. The seventies are remembered as 'the Golden Age' of activism, the 'Real Thing' (Stacey 1997:59) – a wonderful time of active politics now lost to institutionalisation and apathy. The other side is anything but nostalgic. This position characterises 'seventies feminism' in terms of the 'bad ... object against which the subjects of the present measure themselves' (Stacey 1997:59). At this point in its trajectory, the argument goes, feminism was essentialist and exclusionary of Black and Lesbian women's experiences and needs. This, as Clare Hemmings and Jo Brain show in their article in this volume, is often represented as having been challenged by Black and Lesbian feminists in the eighties and ultimately as giving way in the nineties to post-modern 'difference'. Both these competing representations manage to co-exist in the media, classroom and in academic journals. No simple love: but 'I ♥'/ 'I hate' double-think.

Such an atmosphere leaves this book with a bit of a challenge: to write about feminism in 'the seventies' while destabilising some of the dichotomous and divisive thinking about 'seventies feminism'. This was our aim at the Feminist Seventies Conference which took place at the University of York on 27 April 2002. The title of the conference, now the title of the book and companion web book (www.feminist-seventies.net/webbook.html), enables this process, we hope, through the slight of hand of the grammatical shift: from 'seventies feminism' to 'the feminist seventies'.

As we have shown above, 'seventies feminism', in both its positive and negative incarnations, has become understood as a type of feminism. Through this, the 'seventies' develops into an adjective whose function serves to limit understandings of feminism. By altering the relationship between the two terms, 'seventies' stops being a description of a type of feminism by allowing 'feminist' itself to describe the seventies. The effect of this is not only to point towards feminism as something that was happening in the seventies but to explicitly refer to the range of ideas, experiences and politics which happened outside of the now tightly defined myth of 'seventies feminism'. Our hope is that by swapping the terms we will enable ways of thinking about 'the seventies' which can not only avoid but also take on the grand narratives of 'seventies feminism's' successes and failures.

Rachel DuPlessis and Ann Snitow argue that 'amnesia about political movements is not only an innocent effect of general forgetfulness, but is socially produced, packaged, promulgated and perpetuated' (1998:23). You could say the same for remembering as well. So, here are our packages – all bound up and ready for 'promulgation'. The packages are different in form as well as content. The web book includes audio files of the plenary papers from the conference but also articles whose potential was opened by the flexibility of a web format; while the non-virtual book offers short think-pieces, personal reflections and polemics, as well as longer in-depth articles. These packages – the articles in the book and the web book – are, then, by no means all uniform in shape and size, and they serve the 'memory' of UK feminism in different ways. Collectively, these pieces do not simply challenge amnesia by re-inserting 'the feminist seventies' into our twenty-first century political imaginary but, we hope, also suggest what is at stake in remembering.

Bibliography

DuPlessis, Rachel and Ann Snitow (eds) (1998) *Feminist Memoir Project* New York: Three Rivers Press.

Radford, Jill (1994) 'History of Women's Liberation Movements in Britain: A Reflexive Personal History', in Gabriele Griffin, Marianne Hester, Shrin Rai and Sasha Roseneil (eds) *Stirring it: Challenges for Feminism* London: Taylor and Francis.

Rowbotham, Sheila, Lynne Segal and Hilary Wainwright (1979) *Beyond the Fragments: Feminism and the Making of Socialism* London: Merlin Press.

Rowbotham, Sheila (1989) *The Past Is Before Us: Feminism in Action since the 1960s* London: Pandora.

Stacey, Jackie (1997) 'Feminist Theory: Capital F, Capital T', in Victoria Robinson and Diane Richardson (eds) *Introducing Women's Studies* Second Edition Basingstoke: Macmillan.

Imagining the Feminist Seventies

Clare Hemmings and Josephine Brain

In this article we reflect on the idea of the feminist seventies, its implicit and explicit role in shaping a feminist present. To be more precise, we want to interrogate the discursive function that the feminist seventies performs in shaping the contemporary field of Western English-speaking feminist thought.[1] We understand the seventies not simply as a particular decade, though clearly the term gestures towards and at points directly signifies that period of time. For us, more importantly, the feminist seventies needs to be seen as a *product* of a specific second wave feminist linear history, rather than its foundation. In this historiographic approach we join other writers in thus understanding the past as imaginatively taking place in the present, and as securing the meaning of the present.[2] How the seventies is written or talked about, then, is of relevance to us because of what it says about feminist interests and concerns now, rather than as part of an endeavour to set the historical record straight.

We were delighted to see our concerns directly addressed in the call for papers for the Feminist Seventies conference in York. Two themes in particular seemed to cement our desire to offer a paper in response to this call. The first – *How can the Seventies be re-read?* – posed the feminist seventies as subject to interpretation rather than as a matter of bald fact, and called to mind the status and location of the reader in the process of giving the seventies meaning. The second theme – *In what ways are the Feminist Seventies happening now?* – jumped out at us insofar as it reflected our interest in the politics of the present, and allowed for an unfixing of the seventies from the decade of the 1970s. Neither theme wholly encapsulated our approach, however, so we took the liberty of arriving at the conference with a spliced together third theme as our guide, namely, *What work does the Feminist Seventies do to construct a feminist present and to what effects?*

We were clearly not the only people to think from and develop a historiographic approach in response to the call for papers. Indeed, the question of what the seventies signifies, and who its subjects might be, was an ongoing source of reflection, discussion and tension throughout the conference itself. Mary Eagleton's thought-provoking keynote, 'Re-Reading the Seventies: Re-Reading Women's Silence', in which she suggested that Ursula le Guin's *Sur*, written in 1982, might more properly be said to belong to the seventies, set the tone. From our perspective Eagleton's paper provided an ongoing reference point for the argument that the seventies might be thematically invoked or recreated, even where it is not directly named. If the seventies is not being understood as an empirical fact, in other words, its meaning might become instrumental through association, through chain of meaning rather than direct reference. In our own work, we have discovered that the feminist seventies is often implied through periodisation of a variety of types – for example displacement by the more readily identified eighties, nostalgic invocation as either (laudably) more political or (regrettably) less attentive to difference – or through repeated and thus familiar slippages, where to mention 'a more essentialist era' is in effect to be talking about *that* period. Thinking historiographically about such a recent 'time' presents its own problems, however, as was again made clear at the conference. In her paper, 'Politics, Pleasure and Pain in the 70s', Jenny Wolmark noted that she was bemused to find herself 'an archaeological fragment' to be picked over by enthusiastic academics. And indeed the conference seemed at times to be split between the need to remember accurately and the need to question the status of memory. It would be easy to think of this tension as resulting from a contest between fact and interpretation, but we believe it is more helpful to suggest that the recent feminist past is never simply either real or imagined, but is given life in the present through recollection, research, political intention, and competing knowledges that jostle for feminists' attention now. For us, then, historiography is a method for interpreting the contemporary management of real and imagined events of the past; in addition feminist historiography focuses on the political impact of that management.

This essentialism which is not one...

In the larger project that this article relates to, attention is on the modes and effects of representing second wave feminist theory as a progressive narrative moving inexorably from exclusion to inclusion, sameness to difference, unity to fragmentation, and so on. Here, we want to explore the specific weight that the feminist seventies carries in the service of this narrative. The dominant and most familiar attribution to the feminist seventies is of course essentialism, an accusation so frequently repeated, that it stands as justification for not reading texts from the feminist seventies at all (any more). From our perspective, the issue is not whether or not feminist seventies writing or activism is or is not essentialist, but the means by which our contemporary feminist expectation that it is always already essentialist is secured, so that individual writers who can be identified as 'non-essentialist' only count as exception. How is such a 'seamless decade of essentialism' produced and maintained? What form is this essentialism assumed to take, what evidence is given for it, and how is it mobilised in the service of the broader narrative of progress?

The most obvious way in which feminist seventies' essentialism is (re)produced is through unfavourable comparison with poststructuralist feminist theorists. The following example is typical:

> A particular challenge which faces poststructuralist feminism is how to undo the essential or 'natural' conception of the self, while simultaneously maintaining the category 'women' which feminism necessarily requires.
> *Theory, Culture and Society* 1997[3]

13

The writers do not need to evidence their assumption that there is an essential conception of the self that it is poststructuralist feminism's 'particular challenge' to undo, because this sentiment is so often repeated without further comment, and therefore its momentum is thus so familiar to the reader. Poststructuralist feminist accounts of the subject are staged as 'the first' to countenance as problematic an unqualified 'woman' within feminist thought, which has the effect of making difference within that category (the empirical 'women' rather than conceptual 'woman' of the extract) the unique preserve of poststructuralists, erasing any preceding debates about precisely this question. Divergent accounts of that self, as formed through sexual division of labour as compared to the law of the father, for example, are not part of this narrative,[4] let alone the rich discussions about exclusion that have attended feminism at all points.[5] Such streamlining of inquiry means that any failure to account for women's differences prior to poststructuralist feminist intervention is itself naturalised as representative of the dominant trend rather than a position held by an individual theorist. The 'natural' of the above extract shifts to mean *understandable* in this reading. Thus feminism pre-difference can still be marked as innocent of exclusionary effects, since its exclusions were inevitable and universal. This ascription of innocence is in fact key to a contemporary feminism dynamic, since marking a past feminist essentialism as unaware of its exclusions allows contemporary theorists to lament the fragmentation of a previously unified women's movement in ways that would not otherwise make sense. We can long for a lost unity of experience and purpose (now), because we did not understand its effects (then). Nostalgia smoothes away the rough edges of this particular history; an innocent essentialism can be seamlessly integrated into a feminist developmental narrative, recuperated as loss.

The production of a feminist teleology where essentialism is critiqued and moved away from is secured through the weaving in of additional binaries to bolster those of sameness–difference[6]:

> Empirical studies conducted from a range of theoretical perspectives (radical, socialist and liberal feminist) have all in some way affirmed the existence of women's experience as a source of privileged understandings, if not the basis of an alternative social science. Now, however, the deconstruction of 'women' is having profoundly destabilising effects upon feminist theorising and research ... This has liberated a plethora of exciting philosophical, political and cultural endeavours that tackle the essentialism around women embedded in both feminist and non-feminist texts.

> *Gender, Place and Culture* 1994

In this extract the standpoint theory and empirical inquiry (of the past)[7] are contrasted with the deconstructive tools and 'philosophical, political and cultural endeavours' (of the 'now'). Where women's experience was both object and source of feminist knowledge, critiquing the category 'women' means that it is now the essentialism inherent in that (earlier) inquiry that becomes the new object to be 'tackled.' The binaries that this description produces and relies upon are empiricism-deconstruction, experience-text, and knowledge-critique, where the first term in each case is associated with a trenchant affirmation of 'women,' and the second with an exciting destabilisation of the same. The privileged singular gives way to a liberated plethora. The feminist progress narrative represented here is an opening up or branching out rather than a closing down of meaning, so that (sexual) difference as static object is displaced by poststructuralist methodology itself as *generating* (unspecified) difference. No prizes for guessing which feminist mode of inquiry we are called to identify with.

When was the seventies?

But how do we know that these juxtapositions of now and then, deconstructionist versus essentialist, place the 'then' in the seventies? As suggested earlier, work from the feminist seventies is rarely directly cited but instead implicated by juxtaposition. In order for the 'then' of the linear trajectory we have been tracing to belong firmly in the contemporary feminist imaginary of the seventies, the role of the eighties is key. We would like to mention two sets of approaches that become associated with the overburdened eighties in order to facilitate the move from the entrenched then to the expansive now – black feminism and the 'sex wars'. In the case of black feminism, establishing its critique as an eighties phenomenon allows poststructuralism to become the taker-upper of difference in the post-Butler nineties.[8] If the eighties signifies a growing awareness of racial differences within feminism, the nineties signifies the explosion of difference *in general* (the 'plethora' of the previous extract). This trajectory fixes a before and after racial awareness, then, retrospectively coding the essentialism of the seventies first and foremost as one of racial exclusion. Black feminism thus becomes a trope in the service of the idea of a progressive incorporation of difference, such that seventies feminism comes to carry the burden of this critique and it does not need to be explicit to be thus marked.

    While most black feminist writing is indeed directly critical of white feminist writing that does not attend to the complex dynamics of raced and classed en-gendering, what we want to argue is that its placement in the 1980s and invocation as heralding an increased sophistication in the theorisation of political subjects marks the work of black feminist critiques as 'over' and thus as able to be assumed rather than evidenced in work after that point. The sequencing of the following extract works to produce poststructuralism as having incorporated but also importantly having surpassed black feminism:

> Two related intellectual debates provided the impetus for critical reflection on 'the subject' of feminist thinking. First, women of color and Third World women feminists critiqued 'the subject' implicit within most feminist thought at the time, a subject that normalized the experience of white, middle-class, first-world women (hooks 1984; Trinh 1989). This critique stimulated greater interest in the multiplicity of oppression and fractured the notion of 'woman' and her experience(s). Second, a growing interest in post-structural psychoanalytical perspectives (eg those of Lacan

15

and Derrida), as well as Foucault's notion of power/dis-
course, also profoundly affected feminist theory. Feminists
appreciated post-structural attempts to deploy an anti-es-
sentialist world-view, reject totalizing 'grand' theory, and
embrace multiplicity, difference and the 'decentred' subject. (Sarup 1988)

Gender, Place and Culture 1999

While black feminism and poststructuralism are on one level represented
here as of the same era (all citations are from the 1980s) and as having
related concerns, the imaginary temporality we are tracing here is
reinforced by black feminism's location in the extract as *catalyst* –
providing impetus and stimulating interest. The critiques of women of
colour and Third World feminists are referred to in the past tense, while
the 'growing interest' in poststructuralism is linguistically still active
and present – deploying, rejecting, embracing. Poststructuralism thus
imaginatively spills over into the next decade, while the critiques of
women of colour and Third World women are temporally fixed by their
frames of citation.

As much as it is the era of black feminism, the eighties is also
understood as the decade of debates about sexuality, where feminism
is forced to move on from its sexually essentialist past:

From the feminist 'sex wars' of the 1980s to the queer
theory and politics of the 1990s, debates about the politics
of sexuality have been at the forefront of contemporary
theoretical, social, and political demands . . . [P]ro-sex
feminists argued . . . that radical feminism's representation
of women as disempowered actors fails to see women as
sexual subjects in their own right . . . While radical
feminists see 'female sexuality' as repressed by 'the
patriarchy', the pro-sexuality movement sees repression
as produced by heterosexism and 'sex-negativity' – cultural
operations often seen as institutionalized in feminism
itself.

Feminist Review 2000

Radical feminism, clearly taking place here in the seventies, is imagined
in wholly negative terms. By framing sexual politics in terms of pro-sex
demands, radical feminist analyses of sexuality can be reduced to their
focus on repression, and indeed be discounted as sexual politics at all.
This historical and political separation is linguistically reinforced through
a series of refusals: thus radical feminist representation '*fails* to see

women as sexual subjects', and understands sexuality only as 'repressed'. In addition, what are perceived to be the key theoretical terms of seventies radical feminism – 'female sexuality', 'patriarchy', and 'sex-negativity' – are placed in scare quotes, while pro-sex accounts of heterosexism remain unqualified. Oddly absent from the above account is any mention of lesbian feminism, perhaps resonant only in the term 'female sexuality', then immediately erased by an insistence on feminism's heterosexism. Interestingly lesbian feminism is also absent from the pro-sex demands of the eighties and nineties here, suggested by a rather general pro-sexuality movement whose focus is heterosexism, but whose subjects remain unspecified. What does remain is an undoubtedly anachronistic 'female sexuality', replaced by the sexual as well as textual play of the (surely queer) nineties.

Other accounts are equally explicit in their foregrounding of sexuality as key to feminism's linear diversification.

> Whereas the earlier generation of feminist scholars challenged patriarchal ideologies that reduced women's prime contribution to society to their 'biological capacity' for nurturing and reproducing, the new gender theorists are fundamentally concerned with the historical subjectivity of sexed individuals and the embodiment of sexual identity, seen as indeterminate, ambiguous, multiple (Morris 1995). For Judith Butler (1990, 1993), who argues that sexual identity is lived as a highly regulated performance, one is not female; one can only 'do' female.
> *Theory, Culture and Society* 1998

17

Juxtaposing challenges of 'the earlier generation of feminist scholars' with the 'historical' concerns of 'the new gender theorists' consolidates a sense that the former is ahistorical, universalising, and privileging of a female subject. The lack of citation rather ironically underscores this comparison. The earlier generation are generalisable as well as generalising; whereas Morris and Butler can and should be distinguished from one another, and later work from earlier work. Lack of citation is indeed the norm for recent feminist scholars when discussing that 'earlier generation', which we can by now be certain refers to the feminist seventies. The *techniques* here consolidate a trajectory and momentum that does not need to have all its parts detailed: the story is familiar enough for us to fill in the gaps (the 'sex wars' and black feminist challenges) ourselves.

By consigning both black feminism and the 'sex wars' to the eighties, a clear distinction between the feminist seventies and the poststructuralist nineties is secured. Thus the seventies exemplifies modes of essentialism that do not always have to be named in order to be understood as surpassed: the eighties does that discursive work instead. The feminist seventies is at best ignorant or innocent of racial and sexual diversity, or indeed actively exclusionary through its whiteness and heterosexism. The poststructuralist nineties emerges on the other side of the eighties as champion of multiplicity and difference, although significantly an indeterminate rather than located difference – *difference in general.* In order for this fiction to be maintained a number of other binaries are overlaid onto this linear trajectory as we have shown (sexual difference-gender theory; singularity-multiplicity and so on), and different perspectives within the feminist seventies' literature squashed, erased, or deemed exceptions to the rule.[9] There is something ironic about feminist poststructuralism emerging as both beyond particularised difference and as inclusive of those differences, when this narrative requires the (prior) misrepresentation of black and lesbian interventions within feminism as decade-specific. In other words, black and lesbian feminisms must be contained and therefore marginalized in order for poststructuralism to have finally surpassed both (racist and homophobic) essentialism and identity politics.

18

Reversing the trend

There are of course challenges to the version of Western English-speaking feminist history that we have been tracing, though largely these take issue with the value attributed to the successive eras, rather than with the terms of the narrative itself. Accounts which represent the seventies as innocent and therefore 'good', like those which produce the seventies as essentialist and therefore 'bad', may seem to challenge a dominant vision of feminist development, but are actually vital for the reproduction of one of its core mechanisms. As suggested above, a singular innocence is to some extent already written into the linear trajectory that moves from universality to particularity, actively encouraging nostalgia and inversion of judgement.

> 'Then and there', back in the 1970s, we saw ourselves, as many other feminists did, as 'producers of feminist theory' which then informed and was changed by our practice as feminists; and we entered the academy . . . 'to know and therefore to change the world'. Over the period that has led to 'now and here', it has been interesting to observe the gradual assimilation of academic feminism, and the entry

into it of successive cohorts who 'came to feminism' through the text rather than through political practice. One of the results of the passing of time and the perhaps necessary correlates of assimilation has been the rise of a distinct category of 'feminist theory' and a distinctive professional category of 'feminist theorists'. What has supported this is a gradually decreasing awareness of the earlier feminist critique of theory as 'ideas' produced through material practices cross-cut by the operations of power. . . .

Feminist Theory 2000

In this settling of scores, the familiar narrative structure of second wave feminist history persists. The seventies are equally uniform, the eighties implicitly framed by two opposite poles – change suggested by phrases such as 'over the period' and 'the passing of time' – leading to a depoliticised present. Similar binaries – practice-theory, activist-professional, world-text – ground the narrative, but this time inflecting the former with integrity and the latter with opportunism. Through this series of oppositions it is 'feminist professionals' of the 'now and here' who bear primary responsibility for the demise of feminist activism, where before it was a generalised seventies feminism that was responsible for feminism's exclusions. Yet 'feminism proper' needs first to be established as regrettably but absolutely over, as belonging to the 'then and there' not the 'now and here' in order for her careerist sister to take centre stage in the contemporary imagination. Small wonder then that at feminist conference after feminist conference the presumed death of feminist activism is lamented with such glee.

19

In this final example, the seventies functions similarly as an indicator of feminism's pre-institutional naïveté, thereby facilitating the construction of the present in terms of regrettable sophistication.

Universities have clearly offered opportunities to many students of Women's Studies and provided careers for academic feminists. They have also afforded spaces in which ever more sophisticated feminist thinking can be produced. But there has been a price to pay in terms of depoliticization and exclusion . . . Issues are no longer as clear as they were once imagined to be and feminist work may have a tendency to become inward-looking . . . Critiques of essentialism have brought contradictory possibilities. On the one hand, there have been positive gains from the recognition of difference whilst, on the other, loss of the imagined community of 'sisterhood' has led to fragmentation and dis-

clare hemmings and josephine brain

> rupted political cohesion ... We are left with the question
> of what new kinds of alliance might be possible in a post-
> unitary feminist landscape.
>
> *Feminist Review* 1999

As with the previous example, the trajectory is reversed and many of the same issues raised. Clarity has given way to obfuscation, activism to depoliticisation and careerism, and so on. Yet the 'real' of the past is much murkier in this extract. The present is unquestionably depoliticised, exclusionary, contradictory, fragmented and disrupted, a situation that prevents the development of strong feminist community. But the past is far less transparent. Issues were in fact only 'imagined to be' clear; 'sisterhood' is presented to us in scare quotes and referred to as 'the imagined community'; critiques of essentialism did indeed open up 'possibilities', all be they contradictory ones. This extract demonstrates a reflexive relationship to Western English-speaking feminist linear history both in terms of acknowledging 'contradictory possibilities', and in recognising a particular trajectory as fictional. Yet the 'sisterhood' is still 'lost' albeit 'imagined', leading again to an apocalyptic 'post-unitary feminist landscape'. The loss is in fact of the *belief* that there was unity, yet without that belief, however ironic a distance one takes from it, without that imagined history remaining intact, further alliance is deemed unimaginable. For us, this extract is a useful example of the very real difficulty of imagining feminism in a different historical vein.

Our analysis of the latter extracts in this article indicates that consciously thinking through the form of Western English-speaking feminist linearity is not the condition for freeing oneself from its effects. What we have been describing in this article is a framing linearity; it is not possible to place oneself outside it. To reverse the dynamic to implicate the present as exclusionary and the past as pre-difference (if not immune from exclusion) does not alter who we imagine the subjects of those opposed eras to be. Radical feminism and poststructuralist feminism, in all their various guises, remain at either end of the second wave Western English-speaking feminist trajectory. If the present is imagined as inclusive of a general, anti-identity difference, the eighties becomes over-determined in terms of its (marked) racial and sexual significance. If, on the other hand, the present is imagined as more exclusive via institutionalisation and abstraction in particular, the seventies is recast as unified, and the 'challenges of the eighties' euphemistically rephrased as 'the passing of time.'

Historiographic effects

So if the feminist seventies is alive and well in the contemporary Western English-speaking feminist imaginary, what effects might it be said to have? Or to put this question another way, what difference does our feminist historiography make? We believe that the epistemological and methodological significance of the trajectory we have been tracing can be identified in a number of different realms. Firstly, it is reinforced in feminist writing and teaching practices. We have noticed that radical feminist texts are overwhelmingly taken from the 1970s, for example, and usually placed either in further reading lists, or next to a more contemporary article that critiques it in precisely the ways we have been focusing on. Similarly, the Gender Institute (London School of Economics) core course in feminist theory, despite explicitly avoiding a decade by decade approach, nevertheless traces a trajectory from concerns with sex/gender and nature/culture, through questions of racial or sexual exclusion, and on to emergent theories of power and gender in constituting the subject, a dominant narrative that recodes this history in terms of temporality whatever our counter-intentions. In a related vein, the very practice of writing feminist theory reinforces a vision of feminist history as progressive and transcendent of past 'mistakes', where identifying other writers' (prior) errors typically constitutes the basis of argument. Indeed, our own approach in this article might suggest moving forwards from this epistemological dead end, but in doing so does not challenge the reader's image of what has 'gone before'.

A second effect concerns the broader function of posing poststructuralist feminist approaches of 'the now' as having moved beyond both sexual difference and the racial and sexual identity critiques that supplant it. One of the reasons for our insistence on this trajectory as a Western English-speaking feminist one is because of what we identify as its global resonance. The idea that Western feminism has moved from assuming the universal oppression of women to seeking and embracing a proliferation of differences chimes unsettlingly with neo-colonialist arguments that promote military aggression on the basis that women of a given nation or culture need liberating. We are not suggesting that poststructuralist feminism is somehow responsible for the gendering of the war on the Taliban, for example, but that its posturings do allow Western English-speaking feminists to locate ourselves as having *been through* difference troubles, and having emerged the more sophisticated and attentive to difference the other side. It is this feminist location, enabled by a dominant progress narrative, that means that Western English-speaking feminists continue to view women in non-Western contexts as a problem that needs solving, instead of casting a critical eye over the contradictions of gender, race and sexuality that exist in all nations and cultures contemporarily. The difference between our own and postcolonial feminist theorists' interventions might be that we are paying particular attention to how making a diverse Western English-speaking feminist past invisible is central to the rhetoric of racial and sexual inclusion in the present.

We wonder whether it is this realisation of ongoing accountability for reinscription of the process of discursive, epistemic and material exclusion (masquerading as inclusion) that offers the most encouraging note to close on. The understandable wish to extricate ourselves from the desire of Western English-speaking feminist history to mark itself as no longer racist or homophobic seems only to result in a redoubling of its terms. The understandable desire not to be a feminist subject formed through this exclusion most often means that some other subject, or some other time, must bear the responsibility then for exclusion's effects. And it is this projection of exclusion onto Other subjects and times - not here/there, not now/then, not *me* - that frustratingly enough seems to reconstitute the contemporary masquerades that we seek to unmask. It is our desire to be at the cutting edge of time, perhaps, which currently marks us as most profoundly of it.

Notes

1 We have chosen this awkward phrasing – 'Western English-speaking feminist thought' – to suggest some of the problems of using 'Anglo-American' or 'Western' to refer to the complexities of English-language feminist knowledge production. The awkwardness of our phrasing is intended to raise questions of our own and readers' location in relation to all the terms, rather than to resolve those problems.

2 Gayatri Chakravorty Spivak provides a useful summary of the value of historiography. Gayatri Chakravorty Spivak (1999) 'History', *A Critique of Postcolonial Reason: Toward a History of the Vanishing Present.* Cambridge, Harvard University Press:198-207.

3 Examples cited in this article are attributed to the publishing host rather than to the individual author to indicate patterns rather than individual instances.

4 For British debates on the sexual division of labour see, for example, Juliet Mitchell (1971) *Women's Estate* London: Penguin; Michèle Barrett (1980) *Women's Oppression Today: Problems in Marxist Feminist Analysis* London: Verso; and Anne Phillips (1987) *Divided Loyalties: Dilemmas of Sex and Class* London: Virago.

5 Rectifying the historical record is not our intention here, but readers new to the field may find the following discussions of gender, race and difference illuminating. Lorraine Bethel and Barbara Smith (eds) (1979) *Conditions: The Black Women's Issue* No. 5; June Jordan (1977) *Things That I Do in the Dark: Selected Poems* New York: Random House; Audre Lorde (1978) *The Black Unicorn* New York: Norton, and (1979) 'Man Child: a Black Lesbian Feminist's Response', *Conditions* No. 4; and Pat Parker (1978) *Movement in Black: Stories of Black Women* Oakland, CA: Diana Press.

6 The dash indicates both a temporal and hierarchical separation – in this case we move forward from (exclusionary) sameness to (inclusive) difference.

7 So that standpoint theory becomes over-associated with Nancy Hartsock rather than Patricia Hill Collins, for example. Nancy Hartsock (1983) 'The Feminist Standpoint: Developing the Ground for a Specifically Feminist Historical Materialism', in S. Harding & M. Hintikka (eds) *Discovering Reality: Feminist Perspectives on Epistemology, Metaphysics, Methodology and Philosophy of Science* Boston: Reidel; Patricia Hill Collins (1991) *Black Feminist Thought: Knowledge, Consciousness and the Politics of Empowerment* New York: Routledge.

8 The project as a whole emerged from suspicion at the way that Butler is often positioned as 'the first' to interrogate the category 'woman' as the ground of feminist knowledge. Judith Butler (1990) *Gender Trouble: Feminism and the Subversion of Identity* New York: Routledge; and (1993) *Bodies That Matter: On the Discursive Limits of 'Sex'* New York: Routledge.

9 Many of these are of course simply not re-produced in feminist anthologies or cited in contemporary accounts, suggesting that there is work to be done on the role of the publishing industry in cementing a particular version of feminist history.

clare hemmings and josephine brain

Bibliography

Le Guin, Ursula (1982) 'Sur', in Sandra Gilbert and Susan Gubar (eds) (1985) *The Norton Anthology of Literature by Women* New York: W. W. Norton & Co.

Due to the particular nature of the critique offered in this article (see note 3, above) we offer here a list of journals cited rather than details for specific references.

Feminist Review London: Palgrave <www.feminist-review.com>

Feminist Theory Rita Felski, Gabriele Griffin, Stevi Jackson, Sasha Roseneil (eds) London: Sage <www.sagepub.co.uk>

Gender, Place and Culture Linda Peake and Gill Valentine (eds) London: Carfax <www.tandf.co.uk/journals/carfax/0966369X.html>

Theory, Culture and Society Mike Featherstone (ed) London: Sage <www.sagepub.co.uk>

Desiring Feminism, Wanting Ch-ch-changes

Ann Kaloski

I want to chew over an idea that at first glance may seem quite perverse – I would like to think about David Bowie as a feminist icon. While for some readers this may seem, at best, an odd statement, I know there will be many women out there who understand this juxtaposition. I've had plenty of pub conversations with feminists who were in their late adolescence or early twenties in the seventies, and for many of us Bowie is our open secret: his performances weren't read by us, then, as primarily gay (male). He mutated, flaunted, pushed buttons and boundaries, and yet it was all played out on a man's body that did not primarily desire men. This joyful destabilizing of sexual and gender norms was for many of us the precursor to ideas we would later term 'queer'. Whatever our sexual identities – and a few of the women I am thinking of here are, in fact, het – Bowie helped to queer not only our dreams (sexual, creative, authentic) but also our sense of ourselves as gendered beings, as women.

(But he's just a white boy driven by a need to make successful records)

And I'm just a white girl driven by a need to generate links that help make sense of the world. Alison Hennegan argued in her lovely piece about lesbian reading that, as a young and unknowing dyke in the 1960s, she forged connections between her own developing desires and those of gay men's fiction as well as 'high-brow' and sensationalist writing, connections she might never have made if she had had easy access to lists of 'appropriate' lesbian books (1988). So I too, as a working class girl in a conventional family with dreams at odds with her fate, took inspiration where I could. In the fifties my magic texts were fairy tales, and though the princess always ended her life with the prince there were numerous escape routes, and many a doppelganger heroine visited my humble bunk bed. In the sixties, The Beatles and the pop art culture of my Merseyside home hinted at a life (and not only for the boys) that didn't end in the factory or the grimy offices that sustained them. And as the sixties ended I joined the hippy boys in wanting hippy girls (and sometimes we wanted each other).

And then came Bowie. Magnetic, beautiful, not-a-woman but not-a-man either, at least not like any man I had seen. As he flashed his ambivalent sexuality and androgynous body I caught glimpses of a process that not only exposed but unlocked gender.

(But he was glamorous and rich, you were ordinary and poor).

Mmm. But I'm not talking about the talented, sexy, sometime fascist Bowie the man; I am, rather, alluding to Icon Bowie, and a successful icon (unlike, say, a role model) doesn't so much pave the way as agitate the senses. Icon Bowie pilfered our desire and represented it back to us, made palpable. There was something incredibly feminine about Bowie as Queen Bitch, Ziggy, Aladdin et al, and the kind of ironic femininity he exuded disturbed our connections between women and liberation and movement.

In the end, we took 'our' icon away from the man and attempted to spawn a politicised, desiring feminism, negotiated between power and gender and bodies. Without Bowie queer feminism would still have emerged, of course. But, for many of us, it wouldn't have been quite the same . . .

Bibliography

Hennegan, Alison (1988) 'On Becoming a Lesbian Reader', in Susannah Radstone (ed) *Sweet Dreams: Sexuality, Gender and Popular Fiction* London: Lawrence and Wishart Ltd.

Whatever Happened to Feminist Critiques of Monogamy?

Stevi Jackson and Sue Scott

> *Romantic, monogamous love is an imposed law* – the means
> by which we are allowed to recompose the fragmentation
> of ourselves into an apparent whole. So that jealousy comes
> to be regarded as the objective proof of love instead of an
> excrescence on our emotions. So that sex is legitimised, so
> that attraction and warmth and affection can be called
> 'love', which can then be parcelled into marriage and one
> woman and one man come to symbolise an *institution.*
> Lee Comer *Wedlocked Women* (1974:220)

During the 1970s (hetero)sexuality was
identified as one of the key sites of women's oppression. It is now well
documented that the politics this generated entailed both women's pursuit
of sexual autonomy and pleasure and their resistance to sexual
exploitation and coercion. It is also widely recognised that this was
bound up with a critique of the family, marriage and the sexual double
standard. What is now less often remembered is that monogamy itself
was also called into question and that non-monogamy was central to
the politics of the personal, and thus to the struggle to develop alternative,
non-oppressive sexual relationships. 'Non-monogamy' is in some ways
a problematic concept. As Julie Bindel and Joan Scanlon (1996) remind
us, the term monogamous has a dubious etymology (mono – one; gamus
– marriage) and therefore is not precisely synonymous with sexual
exclusivity even in the context of heterosexuality. Moreover it is possible
to be critical of marriage without questioning exclusivity as the hallmark
of a significant sexual relationship, be it heterosexual, lesbian or even
'queer'. Nonetheless, 'monogamy' was the term that was, and is, generally
used to mean having only one sexual partner.

The two of us came to feminism as young women in the 1970s, a time when the theory and practice of non-monogamy were widely discussed and seen as a challenge to oppressive heterosexual relationships – both by lesbian *and* heterosexual feminists. It runs as a thread through many political texts of the time and featured in much feminist fiction and autobiography (eg Kate Millet's *Flying* (1976); Anja Meulenbelt's *The Shame is Over (*1980); Marge Piercy's *Small Changes* (1972) and *Woman on the Edge of Time* (1979), which explored non-monogamous lesbian, heterosexual and bisexual relationships and transitions between them. Yet now, in an era of ostensibly greater sexual freedom, when pre-marital heterosex is no longer condemned by most of the population, when marriage is far less likely to be life-long, when gay, lesbian and bisexual relationships are far more visible, the critique of monogamy has become so muted as to be almost inaudible – or has been transmogrified, especially among gay men, into a celebration of multiple casual sexual encounters (often alongside a single 'meaningful' relationship) as opposed to the possibility of multiple ongoing relationships. We want to chart the origins of feminist critiques of monogamy, ask why non-monogamy fell out of favour and, finally, reassert the continued importance of questioning the inevitability of monogamy.

28

Non-monogamy and 1970s feminism

The idea of non-monogamy was not entirely new in the 1970s, since it had a history among sex-radicals, socialists and first wave feminists – although this early history was almost exclusively concerned with rethinking heterosexual relations. For Edward Carpenter monogamous marriage was 'a prison, which stunts love and the human spirit' (quoted in Reibstein and Richards 1992:221). Early feminists such as Olive Shreiner and the Russian revolutionary Alexandra Kollontai favoured free relationships. In her political writing on love, Kollontai (1972) damned monogamy as tantamount to treating people as possessions and her fiction, especially the short story 'Three Generations'(1923/1977), explored non-monogamous relationships. The sexual radicals of the 1960s picked up on some of these themes – Reich's *The Sexual Revolution* (1951) being an influential text. Simone de Beauvoir was also an important role model, with her non-exclusive relationship with Sartre being seen, at the time, in a positive light.

1970s feminists were influenced both by the ideas of the sexual revolution and by a history of feminist writing on non-monogamy. As we (and others) have documented elsewhere, the feminist position on the sexual revolution was ambivalent (Jackson & Scott 1997; Snitow et al 1984). On the one hand, since the double standard was never entirely eradicated, it promised heterosexual women freedoms it didn't deliver. On the other hand it rendered heterosexual women more open to sexual exploitation, undermining our ability to resist men's sexual demands. Feminists were critical of the ways in which the male left mobilised the ideas of sexual freedom to women's detriment. Marge Piercy (1970), for example, was scathing about the way men in Left organisations sexually used women, recruited them through sex and purged them if they failed to satisfy. She described how women were passed around male cadres and how men used sex as a divide and rule strategy. It was experiences such as these that led many socialist women into the women's liberation movement and fuelled the critique of heterosexuality. Rather than turning their backs on non-monogamy, however, these women sought to develop a more radical version of it that contested rather than confirmed men's traditional privileges, whether through embracing political lesbianism or seeking to transform heterosexuality.

It should be remembered that, in the traditional, heterosexual context, monogamy was never a principle that had applied equally to women and to men. Feminists were well aware that historically 'monogamous' marriage had served to underline women's status as man's property – leaving men free to pursue romantic and sexual relations elsewhere.[1] However, for 1970s feminists, the politics of non-monogamy was neither framed within an 'equal rights' perspective – 'we have a right to our wild oats too' – nor did it simply represent a hedonistic quest for sexual gratification. This stance was not just about sexuality, but also about coupledom and was rooted in feminist critiques of romantic love, marriage and the family. Rather than seeking to share in male prerogatives, the aim was to challenge them: the answer to woman being treated as man's sexual property was not to reverse this by demanding equally exclusive access to a single man or woman, but to do away altogether with the idea of sexual relations as establishing property rights over another's body and person. As the opening quote from Lee Comer indicates, jealousy, the emotional expression of possessiveness, was seen in the context of feminist critique as entirely negative, an infringement of the other's freedom and destructive of one's own autonomy. Monogamous love was seen as individualistic, demanding to be placed at the centre of another's universe, while building one's own world around them. It also led to the commodification and quantification of emotions. To quote Comer again:

stevi jackson and sue scott

> ... monogamy has come to be the definition of love, the yardstick by which we measure the rest of our emotions ... Like so much butter, romantic love must be spread thickly on one slice of bread; to spread it over several is to spread it 'thinly'. (Comer 1974:219)

Comer goes on to discuss how we are seduced by the pervasiveness of the ideal. To aspire to monogamy:

> ... requires a frantic search for a love object, someone who will be a repository for the realisation of our whole selves. The reward can never quite match up to the expectations, but to admit to it is to admit that we are all fooled. So we sublimate our passion by fierce concentration on the partner. If it isn't the perfect relationship, then either we invest all our energies into trying to transform it or we dwell on its inadequacies. Either way, the gates of the trap have closed, monogamy triumphs even in failure. (1974:221)

For 1970s feminists, including ourselves, being critical of marriage and monogamy was not simply an abstract theoretical exercise: it also shaped our practice. Not only was the personal rendered political, but our politics also informed the ways we tried to live our lives. Personal politics were not simply an individual matter, but were part of a collective understanding forged through political, friendship and sexual networks that were frequently coterminous. Non-monogamy became an ideal to be pursued for both heterosexual and lesbian feminists. Indeed, in activist circles, it was often lesbians who were at the forefront of the critique of monogamy since it was seen as one of the defining features of heterosexuality and a practice to be eschewed by committed political lesbians. As Julie Bindel and Joan Scanlon say, this was:

> ... a time of serious commitment to challenging the conventions of heterosexual models of sexual relationships *and* friendships, rethinking previously unquestioned priorities and risking new ways of thinking about and acting (or not acting) on feelings towards other women. (1996:69)

For lesbians this was part of being woman-identified, which involved challenging the conventional boundaries between sexual relationships and friendships – as evident, for example, in Rich's (1980) conceptualisation of the lesbian continuum (see also Leeds Revolutionary Feminists 1981; Rosa, 1994). The political ideal of investing all women's emotional and political energies in women also led lesbians to think critically about exclusivity in the context of sexual relationships, not simply in the sense of reserving sex for one partner, but also in the sense of over-investing in one relationship to the detriment of others. For committed lesbian feminists, therefore, to be too much part of a couple would call one's political commitment to all women into question by privileging the private and emotional sphere over the political community.[2]

For both lesbian and heterosexual feminists, the practice of non-monogamy entailed challenging and coping with emotional responses such as jealousy and insecurity. These were not thought of as natural, but as socially constructed. As the Red Collective put it: 'a feeling, like an idea, can only be felt if the social relations, which contain it, make it a possible feeling' (1978:7). Yet it was not naively assumed that it was easy to change ourselves. This had to be worked at: and an enormous amount of energy was put into this process. The Red Collective, a mixed group of heterosexual men and women, provide a good example of this. In their pamphlet *The Politics of Sexuality in Capitalism* (1973/1978) they discuss the theory of a feminist and anti-capitalist sexual politics and chart (in terms that now seem acutely embarrassing) their struggle to apply them in practice. They saw monogamy and jealousy as arising from historically specific relations within the family and therefore explored ways of restructuring relationships. By 'restructuring' they meant not only practical arrangements (such as who lived with whom), but also ways of addressing issues of power and dependence, the centrality and separateness of each relationship and ways of communicating about them. For this to be possible, sex itself had to be seen as 'an area for struggle and change, not just as spontaneous expression of given feelings' (1978:97).

Thus there was, in the 1970s, a political context within which to think about the ways our emotions and desires are socially constructed, posing questions about jealousy and insecurity and the sociocultural ordering of love and affection. It was seen as legitimate to struggle over non-monogamy and to try to find a way of practising it that did not licence male sexual exploitation, did not simply enable men to continue as before preying on women's insecurities, dividing and ruling (see for eg Meulenbelt 1980).

The disappearance of non-monogamy

Of course the critique of monogamy has not vanished altogether: it remains in some bisexual writings, in gay men's defence of sexual freedom in the face of the AIDS pandemic and in explorations of queer sexualities. It also found a place in some libertarian writings – for example, in Pat Califia's (1981) lamenting of a retreat to coupledom among lesbians and Gayle Rubin placing monogamous heterosexuality at the centre of her charmed circle of legitimate sexualities (1984), and non-monogamy continues to be accepted, if not foregrounded, in libertarian and queer circles. So one answer to what has happened to the feminist critique of monogamy is its absorption into the political celebration of sexual transgression, where it has become dissociated from the feminist challenge to male domination in intimate relationships. Meanwhile, explicitly feminist critique only occasionally surfaces in lesbian feminist writings (Rosa 1994; Bindel and Scanlon 1996), and even less frequently in discussions among heterosexual feminists (Robinson 1997). It barely featured, for example, in feminist debates about heterosexuality in the 1990s.

Explanations for the disappearance of the feminist challenge to monogamy can be sought on two levels – cohort or intra-generational effect and intergenerational effect. It is possible that within different generations of women there are different reasons for this lack of critique. For our cohort (women who came to feminism in the 1970s, who are now mostly in their late 40s or 50s), the ability to develop a critique of monogamy derived from the political moment in which we came to feminism and the availability of a number of discourses supporting such a critique. Also, we became sexually active in an environment where marriage was much more entrenched as the legitimate avenue for sexual expression. Younger cohorts of women have come to adulthood and to feminism in an era of ostensibly greater sexual freedom but in a climate where the radical questioning of sexual exclusivity central to our experience has been eclipsed by other sexual political priorities and for whom, perhaps, our concern with egalitarian and open sexual relationships seems quaintly old-fashioned. Since more recent generations of feminists will have a different story to tell, and quite possibly different interpretations of monogamy, we will concentrate here on what happened to our own cohort.

For our generation, the most immediate difficulties we encountered related to the practice of non-monogamy – in attempting to change our emotions, dealing with conflicts and developing new moral frameworks. But no-one ever thought it was going to be easy – the recognition that our emotions are a social product did not mean that they would be easy to change (Scanlon and Bindel 1996); as Sue Cartledge put it, feelings of jealousy and insecurity 'could not be wished away through political analysis' (1983:173). Alternative moral frameworks were not self-evident and conflicts were bound to occur. These issues were documented in some autobiographical accounts (Cartledge 1983, Meulenbelt 1980), had featured in 70s and early 80s fiction and were endlessly discussed in some more political writings (Red Collective). For some, trying to cope with the challenges these problems posed was 'like scaling Everest with a toothpick' (Scanlon and Bindel 1996:69). Sue Cartledge paints a rather bleak picture of what, in a heterosexual context, balancing two sexual relationships might entail:

> My clearest memory of those months is of trekking from one flat to another, diaphragm in handbag, trying to ap-pease both husband and lover, endless rows, and feeling somewhat like a bone between two emotionally-demand-ing dogs. (1983:173)

Situations like this, however, were often recognised as far from ideal since they were premised on a central relationship and an external 'other' (see, eg Red Collective 1978). Thus for some, the kind of non-monogamy Sue Cartledge describes here would not be radical enough – certainly not for those who, like many lesbian feminists, were arguing for greater parity between non-sexual and sexual relationships. Moreover, Cartledge makes non-monogamy seem a form of drudgery – doing emotional and sexual labour for two men – rather than gaining pleasure for herself from two lovers. Non-monogamy may have caused problems and tensions, but it also provided a means of exploring one's sexuality, avoiding the routinisation inherent in many couple relations and the guilt of being attracted to someone new. Also, in the context of supportive networks of friends and lovers (including friends who are also lovers), it potentially enriched one's personal and social life and could be very self-affirming.

33

For some, however, the problems seemed to have outweighed the pleasures and, faced with the difficulties of changing their lives and dealing with the consequent emotional turmoil, they simply gave up and retreated to more predictable couple relationships. However, this was not a universal experience and even if it had been, it would be insufficient to explain the widespread retreat from non-monogamy. When there was still a collective political will to struggle for change in our personal relationships, the possibility remained open. By the 1980s political shifts were occurring within feminism, which shifted the terrain of debate and the configuration of political alliances.

Lesbian feminists, as we have noted, had been at the forefront of the critique of monogamy, defining it as a quintessentially heterosexual institution. Later, in the context of the 1980s 'sex wars', non-monogamy became associated in the minds of some political lesbians with s/m libertarianism, with the celebration of an individualistic, purely sexual and hedonistic pursuit of sexual variety. This was a problematic association for some lesbian feminists and, for those critical of the libertarian turn, provided a political rationale for a retreat to monogamous couple relationships (Bindel and Scanlon 1996). The pursuit of egalitarian lesbian relationships, for many, became focused on the committed couple rather than the critique of exclusive couples. For heterosexual feminists, this lesbian retreat made it even harder to justify non-monogamy and removed a source of support. Where once we could say 'I may be a heterosexual but at least I'm not monogamous', and thus see ourselves as challenging dominant heterosexual conventions, now the rug was pulled from under us. How could we justify sleeping with not just one enemy but an army (or at least a battalion) of them?

We were also facing changes in our lifestyles as we aged: more domestic and work-related responsibilities reduced the time and energy needed to maintain non-monogamous lifestyles. Even for those without children, like ourselves, maintaining a career involved geographical mobility and thus distance from the networks that once supported alternative styles of relationships. Retreating to coupledom may, for many, simply have seemed an easy option – and seemed to be a choice made by many of our contemporaries – but for others it was simply a process of attrition. Once there were more couples and less singles around, practising heterosexual non-monogamy became more difficult. Not only were there fewer potential sexual partners to practise it with, the social context became less supportive. In this situation it was all too easy to find oneself in relationships that were difficult to justify – as when our non-monogamy turned out to be his adultery. Serial monogamy rather than non-monogamy became the prevailing pattern. For heterosexual women, relationships per se sometimes entailed an ongoing struggle to maintain equality within them – as Caroline Ramazanoglu (1993) comments, we simply became tired of coping with the work this entailed. The tiredness factor, of course, is exacerbated if there are several men to be negotiated with. In the old days, enmeshed in supportive networks the chances were that you knew another woman or two involved with the same circuit of men so that collective strategies – or at least support – were available. Doing it alone was somewhat different.

In our everyday lives we ourselves (and others like us) are now less embedded in social networks where non-monogamy is practised, and as time goes by it is increasingly less understood. There are also anxieties about how, as heterosexual women, we are perceived by others – as being exploited and used or unscrupulous and immoral (if seen as the 'other woman') or as cheated on and sinned against if seen as the man's 'rightful' partner. Today non-monogamy is spoken and written about primarily in the context of 'affairs' or 'adultery' (Lawson 1988; Reibstein and Richards 1992). Monogamy has become so taken for granted as the norm that the only imaginable departure from it is the 'bit on the side', the passionate affair that presages the trading in of an old partner for a new one; where sexual relationships do not fit this model, they are generally simply dismissed as 'promiscuous'. We are back to the situation where a heterosexual woman with more than one partner cannot be seen as committed to any, and certainly not to all, of them. She is in danger of being seen as a 'slag' by men and a threat by other women.

The persistence of monogamous coupledom

It is curious that in an age where sex before marriage, even casual sex, is widely accepted, where couples frequently part, where couples maintain a mask of monogamy without actual sexual exclusivity, that early critiques of monogamy have been lost. Even if we are, as Giddens (1992) suggests, living in an era of contingent 'pure' relationships, which last only as long as they are mutually satisfactory, these relationships remain, ideally at least, monogamous. Lifelong monogamy has given way to serial monogamy and, often, pretended monogamy: according to the 2000 national sex survey, 9 percent of women and 14 percent of men admit to having concurrent sexual partners in the previous year, a significant increase in reporting for women since 1990 (Johnson et al 2001).

While men report more departures from monogamy, women are catching up and there is no reason to assume that women are inherently any more monogamous than are men. Historically women have been more penalised by double moral standards and probably still have fewer opportunities for heterosexual liaisons than men for a variety of reasons, including domestic responsibilities and the tendency of men to prefer younger women, so that women's sexual opportunities decline with age. Public discourses and popular culture, however, remain supportive of female monogamy with evolutionary psychology increasingly justifying the idea that men are designed to sow their oats as widely as possible (to maximise genetic offspring) while women are predisposed to seek the support of a single partner (to ensure the survival of offspring). The idea of men's and women's intrinsic difference is also well-entrenched in self-help culture, a genre of psychobabble encouraging us to focus on the one to one, improving the central relationship in one's life. Underpinning all of this is the individualist modernist ethos of the unitary and authentic self, realised in romantic love through finding 'the only one' – that unique other through whom we will each find ourselves (see Jackson 1993).

Yet despite these potent cultural discourses, a substantial minority of women, as well as men, are not, in practice, monogamous but are likely to claim to be. Occasional 'lapses' are explained away as one-off events of little significance (Reibstein and Richards 1992). Many heterosexuals say, for example, that it is better to 'stray' with someone you don't care about than with someone you do care about and that they could cope if their partner had a one-night stand that 'means nothing' but not if it was a meaningful relationship. We find this perplexing. Do women really want to have relationships with men who treat other women like this? Would they not rather have relationships with people who cared about those they were intimate with? Are new 'meaningful' relationships really so threatening; do they necessarily invalidate an existing relationship? It is time we questioned anew the contradictory, and often disturbing, ideas that support monogamy.

It has become more difficult to question the taken-for-granted character of monogamy because there is no longer a widely circulated feminist language with which to do so. Instead there is an, often unarticulated, assumption that in heterosexual relations it is women who are damaged by lack of monogamy – and that no self-respecting feminist would 'steal' another woman's man. There is a widespread parallel assumption that committed lesbian feminists should be wary of libertarian sexual excess. Meanwhile, although the idea that sexuality is socially constructed has gained wide academic currency, our emotions are frequently treated as if insulated from the social, leading to a failure to question the 'naturalness' of jealousy and sexual exclusivity. In this respect our thinking has gone backwards from the days when the Red Collective exhorted us to examine the social conditions through which our emotions were forged.

Reviving the critique

Feminists in the 1970s argued that putting all our emotional investment into a single 'love' relationship impoverished our social lives (Firestone 1970; Comer 1974). This line of reasoning continued to inform critiques of the family and romantic love into the 1980s and 1990s, although in this context monogamy itself was rarely discussed (see, for example,

Barrett and McIntosh 1982; Jackson 1993). The centrality of monogamous sexual-romantic relationships not only encourages us to de-prioritise our friendships, but also structures how we socialise with friends. Couples tend to socialise with other couples and the dominant ideals of 'togetherness' lead to the assumption that friends should be friends of the couple, not one or other of the partners. This tends to render us vulnerable to the loss of friends when relationships break down, or forces our friends into 'taking sides'. Moreover, it also leads to the assumption that we have a pre-ordained right to impose a lover on our friends. Once we cease to take this for granted, we can see how absurd it is:

> ... imagine the idea of welcoming or even tolerating the presence of an uninvited stranger joining you on holiday, coming to dinner, staying overnight in your home if she wasn't simply taken on 'faith' ... by virtue of her sexual connection (however short-lived) with an established friend you have no wish to offend.
>
> (Bindel and Scanlon 1996:70)

In the heterosexual world the assumption that couples must socialise together is even more ingrained, to the extent that single people become difficult to integrate into conventional social gatherings.

37

In addition to imposing partners on our friends, we make demands of partners we would never make of friends, particularly the demand for exclusivity: the insistence that not only is the relationship special and exclusive, but the thing that makes it special – sex – is something to be engaged in only with that person. The priority given to sex, its status as 'special' is something that should be questioned. It is, we would argue, the root of jealousy and possessiveness, those emotions that seventies feminists critiqued but which are now frequently excused as 'natural' or at least 'understandable'. Sex is treated as special on two levels: as definitive of a special kind of relationship and as, in itself, a special form of activity. The two intersect in that the special activity is seen as the glue that holds the special relationship together and, if the glue fails to bond them effectively, exclusively, if one becomes even momentarily stuck on (to) someone else, the whole relationship falls apart.

We need to ask why this should be. Why should sexual love be regarded as more exclusive than any other kind of love? No one suggests that a woman who has two children loves each of them less than a woman with only one, yet we assume that she cannot love two lovers. Why is having sex with someone other than a given partner equated with betrayal? Why do we call it infidelity? There are far worse forms of betrayal and faithlessness. Why do we assume that a sexual relationship should lead us to being treated as one of a pair, indeed as half a person? It is common for one's partner to be referred to as one's 'other half' or a couple as 'an item' – linguistic practices that make us feel rather queasy. If we suspend the idea of sex as a special activity, defining a special relationship, we can see how ludicrous it is to see the person we have sex with as so different from friends we do other things with. To take an example, a woman has a friend with whom she regularly plays tennis. No one would assume that, if they invited her to dinner or for a weekend, that they should automatically invite her tennis partner as well, and we certainly would not expect her to be crying down the phone because her tennis partner had played a game with someone else. Yes of course sex is different – there are all sorts of emotions invested in sex – but we need to ask why, and why they are so different from emotions invested in other relationships. It is worth reminding ourselves that this difference is not natural and should not simply be taken for granted.

Finally, why should monogamy be equated with security? We talk a great deal about the importance of trust in relationships, but if everything important is circumscribed then there is no need for trust. Trust is necessary in a context of risk. Forbidding something and then 'trusting' someone not to break the rules somehow misses the point. In a social climate where serial monogamy prevails, promising monogamy and assuming that the relationship will end if the promise is broken surely creates conditions for the ultimate insecurity.

Monogamy and Heterosexuality

There continue to be good political reasons for questioning monogamy. From a feminist perspective, the critique of monogamy remains important if we are to retain a critical take on sexuality and, in particular, institutionalised heterosexuality. As others have recently reminded us, monogamy is central to the maintenance of compulsory heterosexuality (Rosa 1994; Robinson 1997). As long as monogamy is taken as the norm, ways of living outside family structures will always be cast as less than ideal, making it difficult to accommodate those who eschew heterosexuality unless they conform to an imitation of the heterosexual ideal. A society organised around monogamous couples does not simply order our sexual lives in particular ways, but also our wider social lives, and informs the ways in which policy is made around childcare, social security and a host of other issues (Robinson 1997). Indeed if the primacy of the couple ceased to be recognised, it would be difficult to maintain the forms of privilege that accrue to heterosexuality (Rosa 1994).

Rosa, writing from a lesbian perspective in the tradition of Rich (1980), emphasises women's friendships with each other, which, she suggests, would become more central if the boundaries between friends and lovers were broken down. Our own perspective does not take gendered relations (including relations among women) as given. Rather we would suggest that if sexual relationships were de-prioritised as the basis for our most meaningful social ties and if they were not exclusive, then who one related to sexually might come to be of far less social significance. Heterosexuality would then lose its privileged, institutionalised status; non-sexual friendships per se, whether heterosocial or homosocial, would no longer be regarded as intrinsically less significant than sexual ones.

A version of this article will be published in the journal *Feminism and Psychology.*

Notes

1 Note that the ideals of marriage based on romantic love and mutual sexual 'fidelity' as the proof of love, are historically relatively recent, see de Rougement [1940] 1983; Stone 1977; Sarsby 1983; Gillis 1985; Seidman 1991.

2 What this often led to was a great deal of public displays of emotion!

Bibliography

Barrett, Michèle and Mary McIntosh (1982) *The Anti-Social Family* London: Verso.

Bindel, Julie and Joan Scanlon (1996) 'Barking Back', *Trouble & Strife* 33:68-72.

Cartledge, Sue (1983) 'Duty and desire: creating a feminist morality', in Sue Cartledge and Joanna Ryan (eds) *Sex and Love: New Thoughts on Old Contradictions* London: The Women's Press.

Comer, Lee (1974) *Wedlocked Women* Leeds: The Feminist Press.

Firestone, Shulamith (1970) *The Dialectic of Sex* London: Paladin.

Giddens, Anthony (1992) *The Transformation of Intimacy* Cambridge: Polity.

Gillis, John (1985) *For Better, For Worse: British Marriages, 1600 to the Present* Oxford: Oxford University Press.

Hite, Shere (1991) *The Hite Report on Love, Passion and Emotional Violence* London: Optima.

Jackson, Stevi (1993) 'Even sociologists fall in love', *Sociology* 27, 2:201-220.

Jackson, Stevi and Sue Scott (1997) 'Sexual skirmishes and feminist factions', in Stevi Jackson and Sue Scott (eds) *Feminism and Sexuality: A Reader* Edinburgh: Edinburgh University Press.

Johnson, A. et al (2001) 'Sexual behaviour in Britain: Partnerships, Practices, and HIV Risk Behaviours', *The Lancet* 358:1835-1842.

Kollontai, Alexandra (1972) *Sexual Relations and the Class Struggle/Love and the New Morality* translated from the Russian by Alix Holt, Bristol: Falling Wall Press.

Kollontai, Alexandra (1977) 'Three Generations', in *The Love of Worker Bees* translated from the Russian by Cathy Porter, London: Virago (originally published in Russian, 1923).

Lawson, Annette (1988) *Adultery: An Analysis of Love and Betrayal* Oxford: Blackwell.

Millet, Kate (1976) *Flying* London: Paladin.

Meulenbelt, Anja (1980) *The Shame is Over* London: The Women's Press.

Piercy, Marge (1970) 'The Grand Coolie Damn', in Robin Morgan *Sisterhood is Powerful* New York: Vintage.

Piercy, Marge (1972) *Small Changes* New York: Doubleday.

Piercy, Marge (1979) *Woman on the Edge of Time* London: The Women's Press.

Ramazanoglu, Caroline (1993) 'Love and the politics of heterosexuality', in Sue Wilkinson and Celia Kitzinger (eds) *Heterosexuality: a Feminism and Psychology Reader* London: Sage.

Red Collective (1973/1978) *The Politics of Sexuality in Capitalism* London: Red Collective/Publications Distribution Cooperative.

Reibstein, Janet and Martin Richards (1992) *Sexual Arrangements: Marriage, Monogamy and Affairs* London: William Heinemann.

Reich, Wilhelm (1951) *The Sexual Revolution* London: Vision Press.

Robinson, Victoria (1997) 'My baby just cares for me: feminism, heterosexuality and non-monogamy', *Journal of Gender Studies* 6, 2:143-158.

Rosa, Becky (1994) 'Anti-monogamy: a radical challenge to compulsory heterosexuality?', in Gabriele Griffin, Marianne Hester, Shirin Rai and Sasha Roseneil (eds) *Stirring it: Challenges for Feminism* London: Taylor & Francis.

Rougement, Denis de [1940](1983) *Love in the Western World* Princeton NJ: Princeton University Press.

Sarsby, Jacqueline (1983) *Romantic Love and Society* Harmondsworth: Penguin.

Seidman, Steven (1991) *Romantic Longings: Love in America 1830-1980* New York: Routledge.

Stone, Lawrence (1977) *The Family, Sex and Marriage in England 1500-1800* London: Weidenfeld and Nicolson.

Snitow, Ann, Christine Stanstell and Sharon Thompson (eds) (1984) *Desire: The Politics of Sexuality* London: Virago.

A Movement of its Own:

The Women's Liberation Movement in South Wales

Avril Rolph

On 8 March 2001, International Women's Day, the Welsh daily newspaper *The Western Mail* appeared with the masthead *The Western Femail*. The reason given for the first masthead change in more than 100 years was 'to court publicity in order to force women's issues into as wide a public domain as possible' (*Western Mail* 2001:1).

This special edition of *The Western Mail*, however, focused only on the achievements of women from the 1980s onwards. Nowhere was acknowledgement made of the fact that women in Wales had been actively pursuing feminist agendas from 1970 onwards and that campaigns and achievements of the 1980s and beyond were built on the work of women active in the Women's Liberation Movement (WLM) in the 1970s.

Feminism was very much alive and well in Wales in the 1970s. It was, however, different in some important ways from its counterpart in England, particularly urban England. Welsh groups were often small in size and had to cope with the difficulties of networking between women who were geographically relatively isolated, sometimes in close-knit rural Welsh-speaking communities. The movement had to establish itself in a society in which traditional trade union and Labour politics, almost exclusively male-dominated, were the norm. As Deirdre Beddoe has commented, 'Welsh women were subjected to a particular "virulent strain" of patriarchy' (Beddoe 2000:180). Massive social change was taking place in the 1970s as traditional heavy industries such as mining and steel working declined very sharply and vast numbers of male jobs were lost. And, of major significance, the Welsh language and ideas of Welsh nationalism also played a large part in shaping the nature of the WLM in Wales.

The Western Mail was by no means alone in ignoring the existence of 1970s feminism. The fact that the WLM existed in Wales at all still appears to be a source of surprise to many people, including plenty in Wales who might be expected to know better. One of the few references to the movement came from Kenneth Morgan, a major historian of Welsh history, who made the inaccurate (and culturally loaded) assertion that 'there is scant evidence that the more aggressive or misanthropic forms of "Women's Lib" made much impact in a friendly country like Wales' (Morgan 1981:352). While this can be seen as not untypical of male attitudes towards women in Wales, it is more worrying that when Teresa Rees, Equal Opportunities Commissioner for Wales, commented recently on women's achievements in Wales, she also ignored the contributions of women in the 1970s, focusing only on the growth of women's initiatives and organisations in the 1980s (Rees 1999).

My own experience, when I began to research the WLM in South Wales, was to encounter surprise and often bemusement when I explained my subject, even from professionals such as archivists and other historians. Where connections were made between the words 'women's' and 'liberation' and 'movement' they were most often applied to those involved with the women's peace movement, in particular at Greenham Common, and the support groups during the miners' strike of 1985-6. Graham Day, in a recent sociological study of Wales made direct links between the two campaigns, claiming that women in the miners' support groups who showed unexpected leadership and public speaking skills had taken their inspiration from the women involved in Greenham peace camps (Day 2000:140).

Both of these movements, the women's peace movement and the miners' support groups, began after more than a decade of women's radical action in Wales. Cardiff Women's Action Group included women from local mining areas, and many of the women who became heavily involved in the women's peace movement in Wales had been involved in the feminist groups and actions of the 1970s. By the time women became involved in the campaigns of the 1980s, there was a well-established, if small, feminist network with an already enviable record of visible achievements.

Given this neglect of the 1970s, in this chapter I hope to begin the process of reinstatement. I will look at the nature of the WLM in Wales, in particular by examining the activities of feminists in Cardiff and Swansea and the nature of the groups which developed there. Conferences were an important aspect of 1970s feminism and I will examine their significance for South Wales women at both local and national level. The difficulties faced by women who identified themselves as lesbian feminists and the significance of the Welsh nationalist movement and the Welsh language to the WLM will also be considered.

Local groups - Cardiff

The first stirrings of Wales' second wave of feminism after decades of inactivity began in Cardiff in 1970.[1] Gill Boden, whom I interviewed in 1996, was one of the three women who started the original group. The group started consciousness raising sessions and, in those early days of the movement, looked towards Bristol (geographically the nearest English city with an emerging feminist movement) and London for direction. Gill also went to the Ruskin Conference of 1970, commenting: 'it clarified for me all the things that I'd been thinking on my own but never had any vocabulary for' (Boden 1996:5).

By 1971 the group had grown considerably. *The Sunday Times Colour Supplement* of September that year had a sizeable article by Sheila McNeil on the growing Women's Liberation Movement and listed Cardiff amongst the current groups:

45

> [There are] about 20 members who want to get 'some-
> thing definite' started. 'I think we are going to have two
> groups; a Socialist Woman group to run active campaigns
> – nursery care and equal pay; and a Women's Liberation
> group based at the university which will be more intel-
> lectual, more of a discussion group. But the two groups
> will complement and combine with each other.'
>
> (McNeil 1971:49)

This remark offers an interesting insight into perceived ways of organising and possibly reflects some tensions amongst the twenty or so women who were then meeting. The focus of the proposed groups could be perceived as an early manifestation of what was later to be seen as the major split between 'radical feminists' and 'socialist feminists', although some writers, myself included, feel that the division was not necessarily as clear-cut as it has often been portrayed.[2] What is clear, and was confirmed by several women interviewed, is that they felt that as feminists within such a patriarchal society they could not afford to fall out over theoretical matters.[3]

In Cardiff there were, in fact, a number of sub-groups (health, education, study, consciousness raising) formed at an early stage, though many women were involved in more than one. As Deirdre Beddoe explained to me, when Community Health Councils were set up she and another woman went to a public meeting: 'I had no intention of being on this Health Council, but if you were in the women's movement you had to put your name forward for anything . . . there was very much a feeling of "we must get into everything"' (Beddoe 1996:10). For feminists in Cardiff (as for those in other Welsh groups, particularly Swansea), the political analysis of women's oppression expressed itself through practical action in many areas of women's lives. The name of the group, Cardiff Women's Action Group (CWAG), indicates this clearly. An office was rented in the early 1970s from which the group produced newsletters and handbooks such as *Contraception/Abortion/Facilities for Single Mothers* and tried to run a telephone help line.[4] The issue of domestic violence and the decision to work for a Women's Aid refuge became central to the group, largely through the insistence of one woman, Sue Harding Sky, who felt that concrete action rather than constantly discussing the problems was the only way forward. She forced the rest of the group to campaign, although some of them doubted they had the time or resources to take this on. As a result of her persistence the first refuge opened in Cardiff in 1975 and Welsh Women's Aid, a separate organisation to the English one, began in 1977. This separation was reflected on by one of my interviewees, a woman who had been closely involved in the formation of Welsh Women's Aid (and other women's organisations): 'everything that I've been involved in, we've attempted to set up separately from England, because otherwise you just end up being part of England' (J. H. 1996:8).

The formation of the Women's Rights Committee for Wales (WRCW) in 1974 marked a different and more 'equal rights' form of feminism, which attracted many members, including older women and some sympathetic men, who felt more comfortable with its traditional way of working, which included a formal committee structure. While theoretically a Wales-wide organisation, the WRCW was run from Cardiff, although conferences and other events took place in other parts of Wales. There were proposals in the late 1970s to set up a Swansea branch, but this never materialised. Many women were active in both the Action Group and the Women's Rights Committee and the development of WRCW almost certainly came out of a political analysis that change for women in Wales needed to be addressed not just through the relatively radical ideas of the WLM, but by attracting wider support to work to change the status quo. Gwenllian Awbery, one of the few Welsh-speaking women involved in feminist campaigns in Cardiff, had previously been involved in the WLM in Leeds. On moving to

Cardiff, she became involved in WRCW, largely through contacts she met through her work at the university. She commented: 'I felt that in Cardiff it was all much more political than campaigning – people chose whether or not they'd get involved in the WRCW or Trade Unions, it was more traditional politics almost' (Awbery 1996:4). Clearly, however, this perception was a result of her not becoming closely involved in CWAG, which remained a much more radical group and one which worked in a way much closer to that of the WLM groups she had been involved with in Leeds.

Members of WRCW were keenly aware of the need to affect change through political pressure and a good deal of work was undertaken around the provisions and the implementation of the Sex Discrimination and Equal Pay Acts which came into force in 1975. But in spite of its traditional image, WRCW also carried out some imaginative campaigns, the most noteworthy of which was possibly their minibus trip in November 1975 from Cardiff to Luxembourg to present the first-ever petition from the United Kingdom to the newly-formed European Parliament. This called for changes in the draft petition on equal treatment for male and female workers, including equalisation of family responsibilities. The women were apparently greeted with some bemusement by officials and politicians, who were not used to receiving groups of politically-aware Welsh women.

47

Local groups - Swansea

Feminist activity in Swansea, the second major city in South Wales, began at the end of 1972 when a few of the women involved in a local Claimants Union group decided to set up a WLM group. Jenny Lynn, one of the founders, recalled that there were six of them meeting by Christmas 1972 and together they decided to bring out a magazine which they called *Women Come Together* (Lynn 1996:12). They worked together on a number of campaigns, including the Family Allowance Campaign.

Unlike in Cardiff, where the women involved in feminist activities were (as they were in most British cities) predominantly middle class, Jenny felt that there was a strong working-class presence in feminist activities in Swansea. In her view, the ideas of the WLM made a great deal of sense to women who may have been involved in domestic violence, or who had little money of their own, in that it provided them with an opportunity to begin to take control of their own lives (Lynn 1996:9). The group gave away their magazine on council estates, in shopping centres, in launderettes and outside schools, and local women of all classes appeared happy to take it. Alison Scouller, then at the university, became involved in feminist action in Swansea in 1974. She recalled there being two active groups, one meeting in east Swansea which was largely working-class while the second, more middle-class group, was focused on the university. But there was considerable overlap between them and much joint action (Scouller 1997:3).

Like Cardiff, Swansea also produced practical handbooks such as *Getting Unmarried* with practical advice on separation and divorce, followed soon afterwards by *Having Your Baby*. Following its publication, the local evening paper, *South Wales Evening Post*, carried an article headed 'Women's Lib makes its mark in the city', in which journalist Betty Hughes described the pamphlet as 'an outspoken document on local childbirth facilities and ante-natal care' and outlined the '"lady liberationists" [. . .] ambitious and far-sighted plans for the proposed [women's] centre' (Hughes 1975:5-6).

The plans for the proposed women's centre were at that stage slightly confused, appearing to combine a women's refuge and a more conventional women's centre. This was eventually clarified into two campaigns and a women's centre was opened in 1979 in a shabby council-owned building.[5]

The question of feminists co-operating with authorities such as local councils in order to obtain buildings and other facilities is an interesting one, which became of major importance in the 1980s with the supportive policies of so-called 'loony left councils' and particularly the GLC.[6] This was a difficult issue for a number of feminists in Swansea during the 1970s, since they had been actively involved in campaigns to expose corruption in the local council, charges which were ultimately proved. But in order to obtain facilities such as Women's Aid refuges, it was necessary to work in co-operation with the council. Women thus had to clearly define their priorities and strategies in this area.

Jane Aaron has drawn attention to the fact that many of the women active in the WLM moved on to organisations in which they became the public face of feminism (Aaron 1994:193-4) and there does seem to be a strong sense that working through organisations and institutions to bring about social change was the obvious direction for many feminists in Wales, both in Cardiff and elsewhere in Wales.

Conferences

Conferences, both in Wales and outside, were one of the main ways women involved in the WLM in Wales met and networked together. Within Wales, conferences on the theme 'Women at Work in Wales' were regularly organised by the Women's Rights Committee for Wales from 1975 onwards and national women's conferences were organised in various parts of Wales. The programme for what was probably the first of these in July 1974 gives some indication of the scale: 'There are 4 rooms in the flat, so we should be able to have 4 discussions going on at once. We may also be able to overflow into a neighbouring flat' (All-Wales Women's Liberation One-day Conference programme 1974). Suggestions for discussion included feedback from five women who had attended the National WLM Conference in Edinburgh and who wanted to discuss some of the topics raised there.

National conferences were clearly important opportunities for many women in Wales to meet other feminists and exchange ideas, news and debate. The movement in Wales was inevitably quite narrow in its focus, since groups were normally quite small and geographically scattered. Many of them were also university groups, which inevitably lacked continuity as students moved on. Consequently, national conferences were important in offering wider perspectives.

The sense of isolation from each other experienced by women's groups in Wales was apparent from an article in a newsletter produced at the WLM Conference in London in 1977. The problems of organising feminist events in small Welsh-speaking rural communities were also only too clear. The article was produced by twenty women from Wales who met up at the conference and obviously discussed the state of the movement at home:

> There is a feeling of 'cutoffness' among a lot of women's groups in Wales. Up to last year there were regular Welsh Women's Conferences between Cardiff, Swansea and Aberystwyth mainly . . . The last conference to be organised was done by sisters near Carmarthen, two summers ago but ended in disaster – the village balked at the idea of being overwhelmed by bra-burning, man-hating feminists or something so they were refused the village hall.
>
> (Marian 1977)

The role of lesbians

Lesbians were active within the movement in Wales, as they were elsewhere, but there is curiously little written about lesbian issues and my perception is that the debates about sexuality which occurred elsewhere were largely avoided in Wales. Gill Boden identified one of the reasons for this silence, explaining that Cardiff Women's Action Group were aware of strong conflicts, particularly over lesbian issues, within the movement in Bristol and although nervous that this could happen to them, as a much smaller group they needed to work constructively together and avoid major conflict. Although Gill did not feel that sexuality was an issue within CWAG, she was aware that a number of women in the group were lesbians but did not talk about it (Boden 1996:7). It was not until the end of the 1970s that lesbians became visible and active as a distinct group within the WLM in Cardiff, possibly as younger and more radical women became involved.

Two lesbians from Swansea WLM group who attended the Nottingham Conference gave a graphic description of the relative isolation they felt as feminist lesbians within their community:

> 200 women present, including two from Swansea . . . Coming from a place where we are isolated from other lesbians outside women's liberation because of our views on role-playing, sexism etc. and where there are so few of us in the women's group, to be among 200 women, all lesbians was a fantastic experience. It gave us a very powerful sense of lesbian identity – when we got back to our group we were much more open with them. I suppose the only thing I can think of that might be comparable would be, say, a black person from Blanaeau Ffestiniog going to Brixton for the first time . . .
>
> (*Women's Liberation in Wales Newsletter* 1975)

Jenny Lynn explained that in its early days the Swansea WLM group was supportive to the only 'out' lesbian, but that they did not analyse the wider issues. In her own case, it was the debates about the 'lesbian demand'[7] at the national WLM Conference in Edinburgh, which made her realise the importance of lesbians in the movement, challenging her to see beyond her stereotypical images and acknowledge the possibilities of lesbian identity herself (Lynn 1996:8).

Difficult as it was for English-speaking lesbians to find a voice within the WLM in Wales, it was almost impossible for Welsh speakers. In one of the very few published sources on lesbian experiences in Wales, Roni Crwydren, in the self-explanatory *Welsh Lesbian Feminist – a contradiction in terms*, wrote movingly of her conflicts as a lesbian feminist Welsh-speaker and of trying to inhabit two seemingly incompatible worlds. There was no word for lesbian in her Welsh dictionary and '. . . my needs as a woman-identified woman frequently did not seem to be recognised, let alone met. Or, when they were recognised, the response was often negative for they were deemed to be divisive in the face of more important issues concerning the future of Wales and its language' (Crwydren 1994:298-9).

For lesbians in Wales, it seems to have been a slow process to become visible and confident as a group. While lesbians in major English cities could find networks for themselves, the small size and relative isolation of Welsh groups made this very difficult.

However, it was not just lesbian issues which were regarded as irrelevant to questions about the future of Wales and of the Welsh language. The WLM as a whole had to work out a way of bringing feminist insights into the political system.

Politics and Nationalism

The movement in Wales had to establish itself in a country with a strongly patriarchal culture. Politically strongly socialist, it had long been dominated by 'old Labour' where women had little real influence. Until the 1997 General Election there had only ever been one woman MP at any one time[8]; following the 1997 election there have been five out of a total of forty.

Women involved in the WLM were inevitably 'political' in their desire for social change, but were not necessarily involved in political parties, though many were. The socialist feminist conferences, which were held regularly towards the end of the 1970s, were attended by women who were members of the Labour Party, Communist Party, Socialist Workers Party, Plaid Cymru or other political parties, or of none. The conference held in Swansea in February 1979 discussed 'The Welsh National Question and the Proposed Assembly', looking at practical aspects of devolution, including questions such as whether control over health and education would add to democracy in Wales.[9] In the event, the referendum over devolution was heavily defeated but it is significant that there was no comparable forum for women to debate similar issues before the successful devolution campaign of 1997.

One distinctive difference between political organisation in Wales compared with England is the existence of Welsh nationalism. Women were, and are, active in Plaid Cymru, the Welsh National Party. There was a women's section from 1926 but its role was primarily 'housekeeping' and fundraising. Plaid was not unique in this respect of course, since other political parties treated women's sections in a similar way.

avril rolph

Welsh Nation (now replaced by *Cymru*) was the 'official' voice of
Plaid Cymru and looking at issues from the 1970s is a depressing
experience. Until the mid 1970s, most issues had what could be described
as 'pin ups' on the front page with appropriately sexist captions. Otherwise
women were largely invisible, apart from an occasional mention of the
Plaid Women's Committees organising Christmas Fairs and the like. There
was obviously much stress on nationalism and language but the overall
impression is one of conservatism. As I noted earlier, during the 1970s
Wales was in deep economic trouble as heavy industry closed and male
jobs were lost in vast numbers. In response many writers indicate a
desire to enshrine the idea of a 'true Wales' – of small close-knit
communities taking care of each other and centred around the chapel.
But that model could be, and often was, stifling for very many women.
Reading *Welsh Nation* throughout the 1970s, there is absolutely no
indication that the women's movement existed. The rights of men in
other small nations (Ireland, Isle of Man, Catalonia, the Basque country)
were often debated, but women had, seemingly, no place at all at this
time.

It was not until the end of the 1970s that attitudes towards women
in Plaid began to change. The 1978 party conference adopted a motion
in favour of women's rights and, following the return of a Conservative
government in 1979 and the overwhelming defeat of the referendum on
proposals for a Welsh Assembly, there was a perceived need to look
carefully at the make-up and image of the party and take on board new
ideas. Consequently, by the early 1980s, feminists had transformed the
women's section into one with a feminist agenda, but those feminists
who remained active in Plaid had nationalist goals as their primary
motivation, which they attempted to pursue with feminist ideas. As
Charlotte Aull Davies explained, 'Most . . . [women activists] had become
nationalists before they were feminists and had subsequently tried to
bring feminist concerns into the party. They either viewed their
nationalism as of greater importance than their feminism or refused to
choose between the two' (Davies 1994:249-250).

Language

Linked closely to nationalism, the issue of the Welsh language was, and
is, one of importance for feminists in Wales. Cymdeithas yr Iaith Gymraeg,
The Welsh Language Society, formed in 1962, pursues policies of non-
violent direct action in a campaign to rescue the Welsh language. Women
were prominent in the society but there is some disagreement between

feminist writers over the role it played in developing feminist attitudes. Roseanne Reeves felt that it had partly hindered the growth of feminism in Wales, pointing out that some of the female language campaigners held very traditional attitudes, though she also noted that by the late eighties when her account was written, it had been virtually taken over by women (Reeves 1988).

Jane Aaron took a more positive view than Roseanne Reeves of the role of the society, suggesting that this organisation, and to a lesser extent Merched y Wawr (a Welsh-speaking women's group similar to the Women's Institute), together with the Women's Liberation Movement and the women's peace movement, had helped to change Welsh women's sense of identity and had given them a new feeling of confidence. She suggested that Cymdeithas' policy of non-violent direct action had had not just a cultural consciousness raising effect, but also, for many women, a feminist consciousness raising effect too (Aaron 1994:193-4).

A number of Welsh feminist writers have made important connections between feminism and the status of the Welsh language.[10] One of these was the Welsh poet and language activist Menna Elfyn, who was imprisoned for her activities within the society. She wrote:

> I eventually went to prison as a language activist but came out a feminist ... I remember pontificating in prison about language and injustice to women who were themselves bereft of language, that is, of a language expressive of the female condition . . . the voicelessness and power-lessness that one feels as a Welsh person is equivalent to the powerless of being female . . . (Elfyn 1994:282)

53

On a practical level, there was a good deal of debate in feminist publications of the 1970s about the need to include Welsh language material. Both Cardiff and Swansea are predominantly English-speaking and many (probably most) of the women involved in feminist activities were not Welsh speakers. Nevertheless efforts were made to produce material in Welsh as well as English. The magazine, *Rhiannon* (subtitled, 'a paper for women in Wales'), which was produced from 1977-9, included articles in Welsh. Women such as Gwen Awbery, who were fluent Welsh speakers, found themselves in considerable demand to provide translations.

Conclusion

It is probably only since the creation of the National Assembly that the legacy of the WLM can finally be seen in Wales. There were (and are) mixed feelings about the Assembly and many women had little faith that it would not perpetuate the male-dominated old Labour style of administration so characteristic of politics in Wales. But a number of women who had been active within the feminist movement of the 1970s and 1980s were involved in the campaign for its creation and were determined that women would play a major role. All of the political parties except the Conservatives (who currently have little power in Wales) have taken a largely positive stance to full participation by women, who have numbered around half of the members of Cabinet since the formation of the Assembly in 1999. Several women who had been active in feminist campaigns in Wales during the 1970s and 1980s have been in prominent positions within the Assembly, including Jane Hutt, Health Secretary and, until her tragically early death in July 2001, Val Feld, who was Chair of the influential Economic Development Committee.

Attitudes are slowly changing. A recent Mayor of Aberystwyth, which is in many ways a traditional small Welsh-speaking town, was a lesbian open about her sexuality who chose her female partner as Mayoress for the year. The local media coverage was on the whole remarkably supportive. While this would be unremarkable in Islington or Leeds, for a rural Welsh-speaking community it marks a remarkable degree of change.

Perhaps the most valuable legacy of the feminist seventies in Wales is that feminist values and ideas have given thousands of women the opportunity to make meaningful changes in their lives. Women who were active feminists in South Wales in the seventies took the ideas and values of the WLM into many areas of public life, and as a result continue the process of constructive change for women in Wales.

Notes

1 The WLM in Wales was by no means limited to Cardiff and there were groups active in many other areas of Wales, including Newport, Bangor, Aberystwyth, Carmarthen, Lampeter, the Rhondda valleys and elsewhere.

2 Amanda Sebestyen offered an alternative approach when she identified thirteen variations spanning the spectrum between equal rights and female supremacist feminists (Sebestyen 1979: Appendix). See also Eve Setch, this volume.

3 This should not be taken to imply that feminist theory was ignored, and there was undoubtedly considerable debate about different feminist perspectives. Jenny Lynn, for example, reported on-going discussions on the role of Women's Aid, and whether it existed as a state-supported 'sticking plaster' or gave women real control over their lives (Lynn 1996:8).

4 The intention was to provide an advice line for women. According to Gill Boden, 'it was all slightly incoherent because we were interested in everything really and we didn't have much in the way of resources' (Boden 1996:6). She felt that the Women's Aid campaign effectively led to the telephone line being abandoned.

5 At the time of writing (Spring 2003) Swansea still has a women's centre, now in its fourth home (with yet another move proposed), the only one remaining in Wales.

6 As Thatcherite policies tightened, Labour-controlled local authorities began to recognise the need to provide services targeted at all their residents – women, lesbians and gay men, disabled people, people from ethnic minorities – and in some cases provided funding for services previously run entirely by volunteers. This enabled paid workers to be employed, but inevitably changed drastically the way these groups were run, involving a need to fulfil bureaucratic demands and creating a different and often difficult working relationship between the paid worker/s and the volunteers who had previously run the service.

7 The 6th demand of the WLM, 'An end to discrimination against lesbians, and for women's right to determine their own sexuality' was passed after heated discussion. Jenny Lynn co-chaired the session.

8 Ann Clwyd, the lone woman MP (Labour, Cynon Valley) from 1984 until 1997, and from 1979-84 MEP for Mid and West Wales, frequently involved herself in feminist campaigns, including the WRCW petition to Luxembourg. Julie Morgan, elected for Labour to Cardiff North in 1997, was also active in women's organisations in the 1980s, and Jill Evans, Plaid Cymru MEP, was one of the original Greenham marchers.

9 It is interesting to note that the post of Health Minister for the new National Assembly has been held since its inception by Jane Hutt, one of the most active feminist campaigners in Cardiff and Wales as a whole from the early 1970s. She is clearly now experiencing at first hand the realities behind the debate.

10 As outlined earlier, Roni Crwydwn has also made connections between her identification as a lesbian feminist and as a Welsh speaker.

avril rolph

Bibliography

Aaron, Jane (1994) 'Finding a voice in two tongues: gender and colonization', in Jane Aaron, Teresa Rees, Sandra Betts and Moira Vincentelli (eds) *Our Sisters' Land: The changing identities of women in Wales* Cardiff: University of Wales Press.

All-Wales Women's Liberation One-Day Conference: programme July (1974) Swansea, West Glamorgan Archives, Archif Menywod Cymru/Women's Archive of Wales Collection.

Awbery, Gwenllian (1996) *Unpublished interview with Avril Rolph for South Wales Feminist History and Archive Project* Pontypridd: University of Glamorgan.

Beddoe, Deirdre (2000) *Out of the Shadows: A History of Women in Twentieth Century Wales* Cardiff: Cardiff University Press.

Beddoe, Deirdre (1996) *Unpublished interview with Avril Rolph for South Wales Feminist History and Archive Project* Pontypridd: University of Glamorgan.

Boden, Gill (1996) *Unpublished interview with Avril Rolph for South Wales Feminist History and Archive Project* Pontypridd: University of Glamorgan.

Caine, Barbara (1997) *English Feminism 1780-1980* Oxford: Oxford University Press.

Crwydren, Roni (1994) 'Welsh Lesbian Feminist: A contradiction in terms?', in Jane Aaron, Teresa Rees, Sandra Betts and Moira Vincentelli (eds) *Our Sisters' Land: The changing identities of women in Wales* Cardiff: University of Wales Press.

Davies, Charlotte Aull (1994) 'Women, Nationalism and Feminism', in Jane Aaron, Teresa Rees, Sandra Betts and Moira Vincentelli (eds) *Our Sisters' Land: The changing identities of women in Wales* Cardiff: University of Wales Press.

Day, Graham (2000) *Making Sense of Wales: A Sociological Perspective* Cardiff: University of Wales Press.

Elfyn, Menne (1994) 'Writing is a Bird in Hand', in Jane Aaron, Teresa Rees, Sandra Betts and Moira Vincentelli (eds) *Our Sisters' Land: The changing identities of women in Wales* Cardiff: University of Wales Press.

Hughes, Betty (1975) 'Women's Lib Makes its Mark in the City', *South Wales Evening Post*, Swansea, 14 March.

J. H. (1997) *Unpublished interview with Avril Rolph for South Wales Feminist History and Archive Project* Pontypridd: University of Glamorgan.

Lynn, Jenny (1996) *Unpublished interview with Avril Rolph for South Wales Feminist History and Archive Project* Pontypridd: University of Glamorgan.

Marian (1977) 'Women in Wales', *Sunday Shrewd*, 1:3, 3 April [newssheet produced at National Women's Liberation Conference, London].

McNeil, Sheila (1971) 'Pockets of Resistance: An operational guide to women's lib groups', *Sunday Times Colour Supplement* 12 September.

Morgan, Kenneth (1981) *Rebirth of a Nation: Wales 1880-1980* Oxford & Cardiff: Open University Press & University of Wales Press.

Rees, Teresa (1999) 'Women in Wales', in David Dunkerley and Andrew Thompson (eds) *Wales Today* Cardiff: University of Wales Press.

Reeves, Roseanne (1988) 'A Welsh Patchwork', in Amanda Sebestyen (ed) *'68, '78, '88: From Women's Liberation to Feminism* Bridport: Prism Press.

Scouller, Alison (1997) *Unpublished interview with Avril Rolph for South Wales Feminist History and Archive Project* Pontypridd: University of Glamorgan.

Sebestyen, Amanda (1979) 'Tendencies in the Women's Liberation Movement', in *Feminist Practice: Notes From The Tenth Year – papers produced by the organising collective for the one-day Radical Feminist meeting held at White Lion Free School, London N1, on April 8th 1979* London: In Theory Press.

Swansea Women's Liberation Group (1975) 'Nottingham Lesbian Conference', *Women's Liberation in Wales Newsletter*, January.

Western Mail (2001) Cardiff, 8 March.

57

Women's Liberation Anti-Violence Organisation

Eve Setch

On the night of 12 November 1977 thousands of women took to the streets in cities across Britain. Their attire was colourful, their demeanour confident, their songs and chants loud and joyful. But they were not celebrating in any simplistic sense. These women were reclaiming the night, asserting their right to walk around free from the fear of being raped, beaten, assaulted and abused or taken for prostitutes by passing men. Colourful and memorable though these parades were, and they will be discussed at greater length in the course of this article, they were far from the only actions that women took to combat and protest against violence against women. This article will look at a number of these activities and consider their significance in relation to the Women's Liberation Movement as a whole.

These anti-violence actions can be related to a number of more general features of the movement. Firstly, an influential element in women's liberation politics was the interrelationship of theory and practice. Women produced ideas through their own experiences and their theories were based in their political activities. Histories on the movement however, tend to look only at published texts, thus overlooking this connection. Secondly, division played a central role in the Women's Liberation Movement. It is this aspect that has been the central pivot in the historiography, for many historians make sharp, negative distinctions between radical and socialist feminists, often blaming radical feminists for destroying the movement.[1] But divisions between women were never this simple. While there were self-defined socialist and radical feminists, what separated them was not necessarily always clear. And different groupings within the sides – for instance the extreme separatist Revolutionary Feminists on the radical side, or aligned socialist feminists, such as the International Marxist Group Women, on the other – showed that the division was not binary. These two features – theory production and division – were integrated since varied experiences produced diverse ideas. Given this, divisions can also be reinterpreted in a positive light, for they were a sign of a vibrant movement.

Historians of feminist anti-violence organisation largely follow the accepted historical narrative on the movement. Many schematise anti-violence ideas with particular reference to radical feminism.[2] Some, such as Rebecca and Russell Dobash and Lynne Segal, do acknowledge that socialist feminists were involved in specific organisations like Rape Crisis and Women's Aid. This said, Segal goes on to condemn the extent to which radical feminists focused on violence as a means of suppressing women.[3] Some of these writers also interpret anti-violence organisation as a practical rather than an analytical arena, concentrating on the ways groups helped women who had experienced violence.[4] Those who look specifically at feminist theory on violence, such as Anne Edwards, analyse published texts, rather than these examples of activism, as others do for the movement in general. In historicising the theorisation of violence Edwards states:

> No comparable [to America] body of feminist work on male violence was being produced in England at this time [the 1970s], though there was the much publicised book by Pizzey . . . on wife-beating and the accompanying refuge movement . . . On the whole neither this nor other forms of male violence against women generated the same levels of theoretical interest among feminists.[5]

She argues that in the late 1970s only two women, Jalna Hanmer and Carol Smart, moved beyond a narrow focus to view violence as a structural underpinning of society.[6] For Edwards, this wider framework developed only in the 1980s.

In some ways she is right. There were few, if any, feminist books which contained a broad analysis of violence against women published in Britain in the 1970s. But writing books was not the only, or even the principle, means by which feminists produced theory. Grassroots discussion and activity, manifested in sources such as newsletters, journals, conference papers and letters, were hotbeds of theory production. Thus a study of these sources presents a challenge to the historiography, revealing a blurring of lines between women on different sides as well as divergent opinions amongst those on the same side. Such evidence shows the huge amount of theory on violence that was produced out of practice and, most importantly in relation to Edwards' assertion, that many different women were undertaking a broad-based, 'joined-up' analysis of violence in the 1970s. At this grassroots level there was a huge body of material produced by anti-violence organisations, including much from Women's Aid and Rape Crisis. A history of these latter organisations is crucial to any comprehensive discussion of feminist anti-violence organisation, but the focus of this article is more limited, looking instead at some different examples which demonstrate how broad grassroots analysis was.

The personal is both political and theoretical

Edwards is right that Hanmer did expound a social analysis of violence succinctly, defining it as 'a major component in the social control of women by men'.[7] And discussion certainly intensified in the 1980s; by 1987 Liz Kelly had explicitly defined violence as a 'continuum'.[8] Yet Hanmer acknowledges that she was not the only one or the first to produce such arguments.[9] Before the end of the 1970s feminist thinking had already extended well beyond the boundaries that Edwards sets.

Feminist journals, such as *Spare Rib*, were prolific in printing articles on different forms of male violence in the 1970s.[10] Even articles which did focus on single issue concerns, such as rape, often contained broader analysis. While earlier articles were less wide-ranging, some did attempt to analyse why men raped, hinting at social meanings. For example, in 1974 Angela Phillips refuted the standard myths about the 'poor pathetic men who are constantly at the mercy of their sexual urges' and argued that rape was about men hating women.[11] But she also pointed to a view beyond the individual, stating that legal change was insufficient; change had to be social, leading to 'a different kind of relationship between men and women. A relationship which is not built out of dominance and submission'.[12] By 1978 other women had developed this social analysis. A Revolutionary Feminist article in the first *FAST Newsletter* also declared that a rapist got his enjoyment from a woman's pain and humiliation but went on to explicitly define rape as an expression of male power and a political crime.[13]

Women in the movement did not simply write about rape, but set up practical organisations such as Anti-Rape Groups. But these groups were also focused on theorising violence. The Bristol Anti-Rape Group newsletter, in 1977, listed group topics and research interests which illustrated the breadth of analysis in subject form, including 'prostitution', 'race, class and rape', 'pornography', 'the Seventh Demand', and many others.[14] The London Anti-Rape Group, which started in 1976, announced that they wanted to take *action* to stop rape,

61

legal or illegal.[15] This action was bound into their theorising, for they also intended to study images which presented women as sex objects to ascertain whether these propagated violence.[16] An article by the group in the anarchist feminist magazine *Zero*, condemned a case in which a guardsman, who had sexually assaulted and severely injured a woman, was given a suspended sentence in order to protect his career.[17] The group did not stop at a demand for his original sentence to stand, asserting that:

> Rape is a means by which every man can reinact [sic] and prove the reality of Woman being a conquered sex, reminding us and them of their power by negating our existence with a total humiliation ... All men are potential rapists, and therefore all women are potential rape victims.[18]

The final sentence in this passage set in print one of the most radical standpoints on rape as pivotal in the oppression of women. Some women rejected this pronouncement, and as a slogan it was deliberately provocative and over-simplifying.[19] But it was a logical extension of much of the theorising that was being done on violence by this time. It was an ultimate description of a society in which rape was seen as a means of confirming male power over women.

By the second half of the 1970s feminists were analysing diverse forms of violence, not just rape, as a part of the social control of women.[20] Discussion moved to forms of sexual intimidation like catcalls, flashing and sexual abuse within the family.[21] But some of these issues had been discussed earlier. While a 1973 *Spare Rib* article did figure flashing in terms of sexual inadequacy, it was nonetheless an attempt at theorisation which took as its base women's experiences of oppression, even if it was less 'joined-up' than later examples:

> ... on a dark night when there is no-one around except you and him, it's not easy to stand and deliberate on whether your knocking knees stem from some deep sexual repression ... or from a straight-forward fear of possible danger.[22]

By the late 1970s, Sheila Jeffreys was refuting the psychoanalytic explanations of flashing which blamed mothers and wives, which had been discussed in the 1973 article, and she questioned those who claimed that exhibitionism produced no adverse effects, for she believed it was an act of sexual terrorism. Rather than being physically dangerous at an immediate level, Jeffreys concluded that flashing was a symbol of a culture in which the threat of violence was used to suppress women, by provoking fear.[23] A piece in the first *FAST Newsletter* on sexual abuse within the family evinced similar thinking. The authors connected together the abuse of women with that of children, and rejected the definition of a child molester as 'perverted'. They contended that there was little to distinguish him from 'normal' men, such abuse being yet another means of expressing male power.[24] The article further extended the frame asserting the need for a feminist perspective on sexuality, admitting that feminism could otherwise be taken to hold a Victorian moral stance. They felt it needed to be made clear that they were not arguing that the innocence of children had to be protected, but that they doubted the mutuality of sexual relationships between adults and children.[25] One practical result of this sort of analysis was the setting up of broader organisations, such as the 'Women – An Endangered Species Campaign', founded in 1978 through the London Women's Liberation Workshop. This too showed the connection between theory and practical activity, since the women in it intended both to research the wide-ranging attacks being made against women and to make women more aware of them.[26]

There were likewise a number of specific events over the 1970s which further illustrate the extent to which women were 'thinking' at grassroots level. In March 1978 a workshop was held in York to deliberate on 'the forming of a 7th demand' for the national conference, the policy-making forum for the Women's Liberation Movement.[27] At this workshop participants discussed violence across the spectrum, from abuse in the media and objectification of women to physical rape, from state violence and repression in prison to mental violation.[28] The statements they prepared for the conference laid down the perceived role of violence in enforcing women's oppression, as did the demand itself:

> Freedom for all women from intimidation by the threat or
> use of violence or sexual coercion, regardless of marital
> status and an end to all laws, assumptions and institutions
> which perpetuate male dominance and men's aggression
> towards women. [29]

Following the adoption of this demand, a conference on violence was organised in October 1978 by the Bristol Anti-Rape Group. Much of the debate surrounding this event centred on the relationship between the conference and Women Against Rape, a controversial Wages for Housework group, and these clashes emphasised the variety of organisations that were at the forefront of Women's Liberation Movement campaigns against violence.[30] As at York, Bristol conference workshops centred on wide interpretations of violence and feminists' activities around them; 'race and rape', street harassment', 'pornography and prostitution' and 'self defence' were all suggested subjects.[31] The specific aim of the conference was to form a national network, to share ideas and experiences, and to create an effective group to press for legal and attitudinal change, again binding together analysis and activism.[32] The subsequent FAST Lady Collective produced the *FAST Newsletter* and the name of the group – Feminists Against Sexual Terrorism – epitomised the spread of analysis.[33]

One of the most prominent set of events organised to protest against violence against women in the 1970s were the Reclaim The Night demonstrations. These were overtly physical manifestations of movement thinking. Begun in 1977, the first march was planned in Leeds and others were held on the same night around the country.[34] These were intended to be joyful demonstrations against the limitations that women faced; women dressed up, sang songs and danced through city streets, often through red-light districts. But the third London march through Soho in October 1978 had a different outcome and consequently gained most publicity. At this march police moved in to prevent women defacing a sex shop with stickers, beat marchers with truncheons and arrested sixteen of them.[35] This led to a campaign to free the women, to protests in court and to women running their own legal defence as a political challenge to the system.[36] In describing the night's events and the court cases, campaigners interpreted the response as a part of the violence which oppressed them. The police, they believed, were defending not women, but male power.[37] Reclaim the Night marches, therefore, like all the events mentioned here, connected a range of ideas together. They were protests against both actual violence *and* its pervasive threat. And they epitomised both the broad focus of feminist theory on violence and the integration of this theory with activism.[38]

Division

As important as this broad analysis was, equally significant was that women argued and disagreed about how to analyse violence and what to do about it. The Reclaim the Night marches, for instance, were not supported by everyone. Some defined them as actions against women in the sex industry, while demonstrators in one area of Leeds were seen by others as racist, for they were routed through a 'black' area of the city.[39] Differences of opinion were widespread in *Spare Rib* and other journals. Some women, for instance, still maintained that the aggressor in a rape was a victim of his conditioning as a man.[40] Relations between diverse groups were not always easy, as indicated in the case of the organisation Women Against Rape. But these differences were a part of the way women thought about and worked around violence. In a different case, a letter from the London Rape Crisis Centre criticised the Bristol Anti-Rape Group for refusing to attend a training weekend, by emphasising the importance of recognising difference. They clarified that London Rape Crisis did not want to be seen as *the* experts since their experiences were different to those of other groups.[41] The issues which caused dispute were as broad as the analysis itself. Varied feminists, for instance, questioned whether campaigning to change the law was a worthwhile activity.[42] The Nottingham Anti-Rape Group defined feminist concerns as outside the law, since it was designed to protect male interests.[43] And a correspondent in the *FAST Newsletter* disputed the applicability of using cartoon-style drawings on badges for such serious matters. Every aspect of a subject, no matter how apparently trivial, was up for debate.[44]

The presence of divisions is widely acknowledged in histories of feminist anti-violence concerns. But it is the differences between radical and socialist which take precedence, with anti-violence campaigns being defined in terms of radical feminism. It is true that much of the discussion and activism covered here was carried out in the context of radical (or Revolutionary) feminism. Nonetheless, socialist feminists did participate in debates on violence in varied forms, as well as in Women's Aid and Rape Crisis Centres. There were papers on fascism written for discussion at the 1978 Socialist Feminist Conference and the January 1979 edition of *Scarlet Women*, a socialist feminist journal, was themed on fascism.[45] The following edition was also framed as an issue about violence. This included articles on campaigns against the contraceptive Depo-provera and female genital mutilation, definitions of sexual terrorism, descriptions of Women's Aid refuges and socialist feminists' analysis of pornography.[46] Audrey Middleton and Al Garthwaite, in the *Revolutionary and Radical Feminist Newsletter*, declared that socialists in this issue had refused to admit that it was specifically men who perpetrated violence against women.[47] But aside from the fact that some of the articles did focus on men, one could argue that in underplaying individual men's violence, this journal had very much placed itself into the thinking on violence as a broad patriarchal institution. More importantly, this exchange emphasises that the two 'sides', radical (or, rather, Revolutionary here) and socialist, consciously interacted with each other.

And so-called radical feminist analyses of violence were never overly simplistic or unified either. This is most clearly shown in the dispute over the wording of the Seventh Demand. An introductory line proposed by Revolutionary Feminists – 'Male violence against women is an expression of male supremacy and political control of women' – was rejected by the 1978 conference. Revolutionary Feminists' interpretations of violence were far from being fully accepted by most women in the movement, radical or socialist.[48] Even if violence was a purely radical concern, and this is at the very least debatable, radical feminist views on violence were just as varied as the topics being discussed. In contrast to the standard historiographical narrative, such disagreements, whether framed as radical and socialist or not, should not be portrayed in a negative light. Far from destroying the movement, they were indicative of organisations which could accommodate many different positions.

Conclusion

Edwards is undoubtedly right that analysis of sexual violence did develop more comprehensively in the 1980s. But in limiting 1970s analysis to only two women and in ignoring the grassroots material, she overlooks the large amount of theorising going on which represented the building blocks of later arguments. Like all other areas in the Women's Liberation Movement, the issue of violence fostered huge amounts of analysis which came directly out of the groups and organisations established to campaign against it. In addition, a focus on anti-violence thinking and activism as a purely radical feminist concern, not only ignores the contributions of different women - both from within the radical feminist camp as well as from those outside - but also downplays the vibrancy and strength of the movement and the intricacies of its debates. Such complexity, belying mythologies spun around 'the feminist seventies', gives the movement a history worth retracing.

Notes

The sheer vibrancy of Women's Liberation Movement debate poses a challenge to standard academic referencing systems, which assume that ideas are a product of a single mind. In order to accommodate this all the references are presented here in an unconventional hybrid form. Full bibliographic resources for material used can be found on <www.feminist-seventies.net/setch.html>

1 For example, Segal, Lynne (1987) *Is the Future Female: Troubled Thoughts on Contemporary Feminism* London: Virago; Bouchier, David (1983) *The Feminist Challenge: The Movement for Women's Liberation in Britain and the United States* London: Macmillan; Coote, Anna and Bea Campbell (1987 Second Edition) *Sweet Freedom: The Struggle for Women's Liberation* London: Blackwell; Rowbotham, Sheila (1989) *The Past is Before Us: Feminism in Action Since the 1960s* London: Pandora.

2 For example, Ramazanoglu, Caroline (1989) *Feminism and the Contradictions of Oppression* London: Routledge, p65; Bryson, Valerie (1992) *Feminist Political Theory: An Introduction* London: Macmillan, pp218-20; Randall, Vicky (1987 Second Edition) *Women and Politics: An International Perspective* London: University of Chicago Press, p233.

3 Dobash, R. Emerson and Russell P. Dobash (1992) *Women, Violence and Social Change* London: Routledge, pp24-5; Segal, *op cit*, p54. See also Bouchier, *op cit*, pp83, 123; Maynard, Mary and Jan Winn (1997 Second Edition) 'Women, Violence and Male Power', in Victoria Robinson and Diane Richardson (eds) *Introducing Women's Studies* New York: New York University Press, pp176, 178, 195.

4 Bouchier, *op cit*, pp83, 123, 141-3; Cliff, Tony (1984) *Class Struggle and Women's Liberation: 1640 to the present day* London: Bookmarks, pp177-8; Pugh, Martin (2000) *Women and the Women's Movement in Britain, 1914-1999* London: Macmillan, pp325-6.

5 Edwards, Anne (1987) 'Male Violence in Feminist Theory: an Analysis of the Changing Conceptions of Sex/Gender Violence and Male Domination', in Jalna Hanmer and Mary Maynard (eds) *Women, Violence and Social Control* New Jersey: Humanities Press International, p21. Edwards admits that a focus on sources other than published texts might present a different picture. See also Hanmer, Jalna (1978) 'Violence and the Social Control of Women', in Gary Littlejohn et al (eds) *Power and the State* London: Croomhelm, pp217-38; Hanmer, Jalna (1979) 'Male Violence and the Social Control of Women', *Catcall*, no. 9 (March), pp21-6; Bryson, *op cit*, pp217-21; Tong, Rosemarie (1989) *Feminist Thought: A Comprehensive Introduction* Sydney: Unwin Hymen, pp110-22; Eisenstein, Hester (1984) *Contemporary Feminist Thought* London: Unwin, pp27-34, 107-24; Ramazanoglu, *op cit*, pp65-8, 165-9.

6 See also Kelly, Liz (1988) *Surviving Sexual Violence* Cambridge: Polity, pp2, 24, 71; Bryson, *op cit*, p218; cf Walby, Sylvia (1986) *Patriarchy at Work* Minneapolis: University of Minnesota Press, pp62-6.

7 Hanmer, *op cit*, pp217-20, 223-9, 233.

8 Kelly, *op cit*, pp27, 34, 156-7. See also Kelly, Liz (1987) 'The Continuum of

Sexual Violence', in Hanmer and Maynard, *op cit*, pp46-60; Maynard and Winn, *op cit*, pp175-6; Leeds Revolutionary Feminist Group (nd 1979?) 'Some Thoughts on Male Violence as Social Control', *Revolutionary and Radical Feminist Newsletter* [subsequently *Rev/Radnl*], no. 3, pp2-3; Hanmer, Jalna, Cathy Lunn, Sheila Jeffreys and Sandra McNeill (nd 1977?), 'Sex Class - Why it is important to call women a class', *Scarlet Women*, no. 5, pp8-10; Feminist Library, Special Collection 2, Box 2, Zadie, 'Male Violence as Social Control'; Feminist Library, Special Collection 2, Box 2, German, Siva (1978) 'What is Male Supremacy?'; Segal, *op cit*, pp102-3.

9 Hanmer, Jalna (1985) 'Violence to Women: From Private Sorrow to Public Issue', in Georgina Ashworth and Lucy Bonnerjea (eds) *The Invisible Decade: UK Women and the UN Decade, 1976-1985* Aldershot: Gower, pp141, 147.

10 Rickford, Frankie (1978?) 'War and Peace', *Red Rag*, p28; Smart, Carol and Barry Smart 'Accounting for Rape. Reality and myth in press reporting', in Carol Smart and Barry Smart (eds) *Women, Sexuality and Social Control* London: Routledge, pp91-6, 100-2.

11 Phillips, Angela (1974) 'Rape', *Spare Rib*, no. 20 (February), p30. See also Feminist Archive Bristol [subsequently FAB], Bristol ARG Box, Shirley Martin, Bristol ARG, letter (24th June 1979).

12 Phillips, *op cit*, p31; Phillips, Angela (1973) 'Battered Women: How to Use the Law', *Spare Rib*, no. 17 (November), p32. See also FAB, Rape/RTN Box, 'RTN - Torchlight Procession' (26 February 1981?), pp2-3.

13 Anon (nd) 'Towards a Revolutionary Feminist Analysis of Rape', *FAST Newsletter*, no. 1, p14.

14 Bristol ARG, *Bristol ARG Newsletter* (September 1977), pp1-2.

15 *London Women's Liberation Workshop Newsletter* [subsequently *LWLWnl*], no. 45 (27 October 1976); Rape Action Group (1978) 'Rape', *Rev/Radnl*, no. 1? (September), p16.

16 *LWLWnl*, no. 5 (9 March 1977), no. 32 (5 October 1977).

17 Rape Crisis Centre (1978) *Second Report* London (30 April), p9; FAB, Bristol ARG Box, C. Sheldon, letter (29 June 1977).

18 Rape Group (1977) 'Against Rape', *Zero*, no. 2 (August), p1. See also 'Revolutionary Feminist Analysis of Rape', p15.

19 Segal, *op cit*, pp36-7; Coote and Campbell, *op cit*, p224; Rowbotham, *op cit*, p253.

20 Anon (1973) 'Are Fathers Really Necessary?', *Shrew*, vol. 5, no. 2 (April), pp6-8; National Council for Civil Liberties (1976) *Sexual Offences: Evidence to the Criminal Law Revision Committee,* Report no. 13 (Revised Edition, March), pp15-17; cf Webb, Vicky (nd, 1979?) 'Abolition of the Age of Consent - or the Liberation of Sexual Aggression', *Rev/Radnl*, no. 3, pp8-11.

21 See also Overfield, Kathy (nd, 1979?) 'On the Crippling of the Female Foot: Notes on the Widespread Customs of Twentieth-Century Europe', *Rev/Radnl*, no. 3, pp12-14; Anon (1971) 'A Treadmill Disguised as a Merry-go-Round', *Shrew*, vol. 3, no. 2 (March), pp11-12.

22 Wilce, Hilary (1973) 'Things that go Flash in the Night', *Spare Rib*, no. 10 (April), p31.

23 Jeffreys, Sheila (nd) 'Indecent Exposure', *FAST Newsletter*, no. 1, pp7-9. See also McNeill, Sandra 'Flashing: Its Effect on Women' and Stanko, Elizabeth A. 'Typical Violence, Normal Precaution: Men, Women and Interpersonal Violence in England, Wales, Scotland and the USA', in Hanmer and Maynard, *op cit*, pp94-5, 134.

24 Nottingham Action Against Rape (nd), *FAST Newsletter*, p5.

25 *Ibid*, p6.

26 'Notes Taken at a Meeting for Women who Have decided Men are the Enemy to Discuss Strategy', *Rev/Radnl*, no. 1? (September 1978), pp4-7; *LWLWnl*, no. 71 (30 June 1978), no. 74 (21 July 1978), no. 77 (9 August 1978).

27 FAB, Bristol ARG Box, 'Notes from the Yorkshire Region Violence Against Women Workshop' (March 1978).

28 *Ibid*.

29 See also FAB, Rape/RTN Box, Malos, Ellen (1978?) 'Violence Against Women'; Fawcett Library, Amanda Sebastyen Conference Box, Malos, Ellen and Frankie Rickford (nd) 'Notes on a Seventh Demand from Bristol Women's Aid and Anti-Rape group'; FAB, Rape/RTN Box, Dunmore, Helen (1978?) 'The Myth of Male Protection and the reality of Male Violence', p2; Dobash and Dobash, *op cit*, p25; Hanmer, *op cit*, pp141-2.

30 The arguments between the groups centred around WAR's take-over of the conference. See FAB, Bristol ARG Box, London RCC, Postcard to Bristol ARG (14 October 1978).

31 FAB, Bristol ARG Box, Bristol ARG, 'Women's Liberation ARG Conference,

eve setch

October 14th-15th, Suggested workshops' (nd); Rickford (1978?) 'War and Peace', *Red Rag*, pp28-9.

32 FAB, Bristol ARG Box, Bristol ARG, letter (20 July 1978).

33 'Yorkshire Region'; FAB, WAVAW/FAST box, The FAST Lady Collective (nd, 1978?) 'letter – FAST NEWS. Feminists Against Sexual Terrorism'. Some thought that the name 'FAST Lady' was problematic, since its connotations were not yet divorced enough from their context to avoid the sexual innuendo that they were supposed to be fighting. See Jennings, Paula and aspen (1979) letters, *FAST Newsletter*, no. 2 (April), pp16, 18-19.

34 Anon (1977) 'Germany: Reclaiming the night', *Spare Rib*, no. 61 (August), p21; *LWLWnl*, no. 32 (5 October 1977), no. 35 (26 October 1977), no. 37 (2 November 1977); Coote and Campbell, *op cit*, p42; Neustatter, Angela (1989) *Hyenas in Petticoats: A Look at Twenty Years of Feminism* London: Harrap, p48; FAB, Bristol ARG Box, Women in Leeds (1977) 'Torchlight Procession 12 November 1977'; FAB, Bristol ARG Box, Leeds, 'Press Release – Women Reclaim the Night' (12 November 1977); *LWLWnl*, no. 50 (1 February 1978), no. 51 (8 February 1978), no. 73 (14 July 1978), no. 74 (21 July 1978); FAB, Bristol ARG Box, Bristol Women's Liberation Group (1977) 'Reclaim the Night' (12 November); Anon (1978) 'We will walk without fear', *Spare Rib*, no. 66 (January), pp22-3.

70

35 *LWLWnl*, no. 41 (7 December 1977), no. 56 (15 March 1978), no. 39 (23 November 1977). See also Brackx, Anny (1979) 'Male Violence Female Dilemma', *Spare Rib*, no. 78 (January), p9.

36 FAB, Rape/RTN Box, Soho Sixteen Support Sisterhood (1978?) 'The Soho Sixteen and Reclaim the Night'. See also Astra, *LWLWnl*, no. 95 (8 November 1978), no. 96 (18 November 1978), no. 97 (22 November 1978), no. 107 (15 February 1979), no. 114 (4 April 1979), no. 116 (18 April 1979).

37 Soho Sixteen Support Sisterhood, 'Soho Sixteen'; FAB, Rape/RTN Box, Sally (1979) 'Reclaim the Night' (9 September); *LWLWnl*, no. 101 (? January 1979), no. 107 (15 February 1979), no. 109 (29 February 1979), no. 111 (14 March 1979), no. 114 (4 April 1979), no. 120 (17 May 1979), no. 122 (29 May 1979), no. 141 (17 October 1979); Collings, Sally (1979) 'Soho 16: "Police Lied"', *Spare Rib*, no. 83 (June), p13. Two more women were fined, see Webb, Andrea and Janie Faychild (1979) 'Soho 16: Trials Continue', *Spare Rib*, no. 89 (December), p16.

38 There was a fourth march in 1979, Anon (1979) 'Retaliation or Celebration?', *Spare Rib*, no. 80 (March), p13.

39 English, Deidre, Amber Hollibaugh and Gayle Rubin (1982) 'Talking Sex: A Conversation on Sexuality and Feminism', *Feminist Review*, no. 11 (Summer),

p45; Crewe, Biddy (nd, 1978?) 'feministsocialist', *Red Rag*, no. 13, p5; Bhavani, Kum-Kum and Margaret Coulson (1986) 'Transforming Socialist-Feminism: The Challenge of Racism', *Feminist Review*, no. 23 (Summer), p84; Feminist Library, Special Collection 2, Box 2, North London WARF, 'For Socialist Feminist Conference, January 1978', pp1-2; McDiarmid, Paula (1978) letter, *Spare Rib*, no. 67 (February), p4; Segal, *op cit*, p63; cf Leeds Reclaim the Night Group (1978) 'Reclaim the Night', *Scarlet Women*, no. 6/7 (April), p45.

40 Dollar, Ruth (1976) 'From rapists to rabbits', *Spare Rib*, no. 48 (July), p5. See also Middelton, Liz (1975) RAP Women and Crime Group, 'Rape', *Spare Rib*, no. 39 (September), p5; *LWLWnl*, no. 101 (2 July 1975), no. 30 (7 July 1976).

41 FAB, Bristol ARG Box, RCC, London ARG, letter (8 February 1979). See also FAB, Bristol ARG Box, Bristol ARG, letter (1979).

42 McCann, Kathryn (1985) 'Battered women and the law: the limits of the legislation', in Julia Brophy and Carol Smart (eds) *Women in Law: Explorations in Law, Family and Sexuality* London: Routledge, pp71, 73, 84-92; Bryson, *op cit*, pp95-6.

43 Nottingham Action Against Rape (nd), *FAST Newsletter*, p3.

44 Sheldon, Caroline and Kathryn McIndoe (1979) letter, *FAST Newsletter*, no. 2 (April), p16.

45 For example, North London WARF, 'Socialist Feminist Conference'; Feminist Library, Special Collection 2, Box 2, Ailsa (1978) Lancaster Women and Socialism Group, 'The Women's Movement and the Struggle against Fascism' (Manchester); *Scarlet Women*, no. 9 (January); Crewe, *op cit*, p5; Rickford (1978?) 'War and Peace', *Red Rag*, pp28-9; Segal, *op cit*, p54.

46 See *Scarlet Women*, no. 10 (December 1979).

47 Middleton, Audrey and Al Garthwaite (nd, 1979?) 'Review of the Violence issue of *Scarlet Women*', *Rev/Radnl*, no. 3, pp17-19.

48 Malos and Rickford, *op cit*.

'It Changed My Life'
Betty Friedan and *The Feminine Mystique*

Judy Giles

I first encountered Betty Friedan's *The Feminine Mystique* in 1983, twenty years after its first publication. At the time I was living in a suburban market town and combining motherhood with part-time work of various sorts. I was completely persuaded by Friedan's analysis of women's oppression in suburban domesticity and identified wholeheartedly with her discontented suburban housewives. All I had to do, I reasoned, to become a liberated woman, was to throw off the shackles of domesticity and throw out the women's magazines. I proceeded to propound Friedan's ideas with evangelical zeal to many women I knew. Not surprisingly I met with scepticism and hostility. Most of the women I encountered had had little formal education. At the same time most of them were well aware of the tensions inherent in the feminine ideal, even if they did not articulate these in the new language I had acquired from my reading of Friedan. All of them were struggling, as most of us do throughout our lives in different ways, to resolve the tension between the desire for individual self-fulfilment and the equally powerful desire for stability, security and belonging. I followed the route advocated by Friedan – education, education, education – and yes, it did change my life for the better. I completed a degree course followed by a doctorate in Women's Studies in which I explored historical understandings of domesticity for working-class women. But for many of the women I knew, this kind of education was neither a desirable nor a viable option. Instead they preferred to negotiate the suburban culture of domesticity within which they lived, finding ways of enabling it to give meaning and dignity to their lives.

Since then I have gradually developed a more critical stance towards Friedan's thinking. Her ideas were drawn from post-war intellectual theories that understood modernity as antithetical to individual agency and 'uniqueness', making people conformist and passive.[1] She was radical in using such theories to understand the particular situation of women. However, her focus on suburban domesticity as the only site of women's oppression privileged white, college-educated women and rendered in-visible the injuries of class and race. My attempt to convince other women that 'leaving home' was the route to liberation was doomed because for many women suburban domesticity does not have the same meanings as it did for Friedan or myself at that time. The mundane spaces of everyday life – the home and the suburb – are valued precisely because they offer familiarity and comfort. Millions of women gain pleasure from creating such spaces, spaces in which children can grow up safely. While, of course, suburban domesticity can be confining, tedious, even a place of violence and abuse, Friedan's representation of suburban housewives as one-dimensional, 'neurotic', passive dupes denied such women the complex psychology bestowed on women like herself. At the same time, Friedan's analysis also ensured that it would be many years before femi-nism began to explore precisely what it is about suburban domesticity that appeals to so many women.

My initial enthusiasm for *The Feminine Mystique* was replaced with an-ger. How could she deny the experience of all those who lived different kinds of lives? Nor were the lives of suburban housewives as empty as she tries to suggest. There were (and are) communities where political discussion and action were integrated into the everyday experiences of women and men in their homes, in the local shops, in the neighbourhood and in the community organisations that flourished in suburban areas. In part my own research is committed to telling the stories of the women who are dismissed in her account. Yet, at the same time, I owe Friedan an enormous debt. *The Feminine Mystique* acted as a wake-up call in ways that a more balanced account might not have done and, of course, her forceful arguments have offered me a different position from which to view the lives and experiences of so-called 'ordinary' women.

Note

1 For a further discussion of this see my forthcoming (2003) *The Parlour and the Suburb: Domestic identities, gender, class and modernity* Oxford: Berg Publishers.

'Challenging the State We're In'

Conflicting Feminist Identities in 'Troubled' Northern Ireland

Myrtle Hill

The emergence of the women's movement in Ireland as elsewhere was associated with Second Wave feminism and the wider Civil Rights movement of the late 1960s. However, rather than the 'Feminist Seventies', the decade there is remembered as a time when the 'Troubles' were at their bloody height. Women's activism in Northern Ireland was affected by, and itself impacted on, broader movements for social justice in the region. While disagreement about methods and principles was not uncommon amongst women activists, the ongoing political and military struggle heightened existing differences and injected a sense of urgency and emotion into all proceedings. In writing this paper I originally set out to explore the relationships between a range of women activists and organisations operating in Northern Ireland during the seventies, with two major aims. Firstly, to consider the extent to which both the contemporary and historical focus on the 'Troubles' has served to undermine the actions and achievements of women engaged in more specifically 'feminist' actions. Secondly, while the experiences of nationalist women have been to the fore of recent feminist historical research, I was concerned to examine and assess the contributions made by Protestant women, to question the perception that they were largely absent from this stage of the feminist debate, and to explore the reasons for their lack of visibility. Carrying out the research, however, I was struck by what this story – or more accurately, these stories – had to tell us about feminism then and now, in terms of both theory and practice. Despite the very real difficulties it poses, postmodernism has raised important questions and made useful points concerning the assumptions of traditional feminist theory, helping us to see that subject positions are multiple, and that shared womanhood does not necessarily equate with shared experience. And that while the notion of emancipation is fundamental to feminism, specific socially and culturally produced gender discourses will impact on different women differently, and other discourses besides those of gender will affect subject positions (Yuval-Davis 1997:120).

It is necessary to preface a discussion of the women's movement with a brief overview of the late 1960s Civil Rights movement. It is now widely accepted that successive Unionist governments, perceiving the state of Northern Ireland to be under threat from both the Republic of Ireland and from nationalists within its borders, survived and strengthened their position through a range of discriminatory practices. This included gerrymandering of the voting system, control of jobs, education, housing and other services. What is less often acknowledged, however, is the role of women activists in the early protests of the 1960s. Issues relating to housing particularly impacted on family life, with young Catholic couples frequently beginning their married lives with little hope of renting a place of their own. The problem was not uniform across the six counties, but from the early 1960s local newspapers in Dungannon were reporting on families living for years with their in-laws, or in

> rat-infested quarters and of as many as eight Catholic couples living in one house where they shared two cookers and two toilets for a rent of £27 per week.
>
> (Shannon 1995:239)

Given the impact on their daily lives, it is not surprising that it was women who took the initiative in demanding change in local housing policy. As one County Tyrone woman put it, of all the problems facing Catholics, discrimination in housing 'was the sorest, because it was always with you' (O'Connor 1993:182). In May 1963, a group of forty young Catholic housewives in Dungannon challenged their local council with a petition, and later took their protest onto the streets. The angry, pram-pushing women were given a significant degree of media coverage and their actions encouraged others to become involved in local politics. Women were also very much to the forefront in the subsequent formation of the Homeless Citizens' League (1963) and the Campaign for Social Justice (1964) and began to stand in local council elections, 'playing a significant role in heightening the Catholic sense of grievance and in preparing large segments of the northern Catholic community to move beyond personal and local grievances to embrace the broader political ideology of civil rights' (Shannon 1995:241). With the formation of the Northern Ireland Civil Rights Association in February 1967, the campaign broadened its base and its demands and, by attracting international attention and eventually prompting a constitutional crisis, entered the history books. However, with the exception of Bernadette Devlin – who became renowned as the youngest ever MP – women's experiences and contributions to the early stages of the struggle are omitted from both narratives and analyses of the period. The men who fronted the Civil Rights movement – politicians such as John Hume, Austin Currie and Seamus Mallon – are usually credited with raising all of the issues, while women have been effectively written out of the story.

Remembering this early period of activism, Inez McCormack, who spent much of her time in the office of the Civil Rights movement, claimed that, in that movement, 'apart from Bernadette, women did the typing. Feminism hadn't hit yet' (McKay 2000:357). This is disputed by another Civil Rights activist, who relates detailed accounts of a wide range of dangerous, international and local activities carried out during these years (Interview with author, May 2002). Clearly, more research needs to be carried out on this turbulent period of the history of the north of Ireland. Women were soon, however, to find themselves at the very centre of civil unrest. When the army imposed a 34-hour-long curfew on the Falls Road on 3 July 1970, broken only by a 2-hour 'shopping' break, hundreds of women from outside the area collectively intervened. Knowing there was a shortage of food on the Falls, they marched onto the road; Marie Moore, from the nearby Clonard, and later to become a Sinn Fein Councillor and deputy Mayor of Belfast, was one of those involved. She remembered:

> It was unbelievable the number who came. Most had a
> bottle of milk, bread, tins of food, nappies, whatever they
> had in their houses. One woman brought sticking plaster
> and germolene. (Sinn Fein Women's Department 1991)

It is also alleged that arms were concealed in some of the prams being pushed. The invasion of women's traditional domestic space by British soldiers searching for men, arms and ammunition in working-class nationalist areas also led to the collective resistance of women. With men vulnerable to arrest or harassment when on the streets, women banded together in 'hen patrols', and took up what became a well-known strategy of banging bin lids, 'on a rota basis', to warn of army incursions into the area. Allen Feldman points out that, 'such community-based resistance is centred on women as defenders of the neighbourhood, an expansion of their role as the defenders of the domestic space'

(Feldman 1991:96). While feminist theorists have long debated the rigidity of the public/private divide, many writers and commentators still readily assume women's place in the domestic realm. There is no doubt, however, that neighbourhood solidarity was a necessary response to the threat posed by the British army. This situation reached a climax in August 1971 with the introduction of internment, when 342 men were 'lifted' in dawn raids and imprisoned without trial. The removal of so many men from their families proved life-changing for whole communities of women. Mothers were left with the sole responsibility of providing for, disciplining and caring for their children, and with little choice but to battle for their economic survival:

> They were suddenly on their own, forced to cope, to be-
> come social security claimants in their own right,
> organising family care around prison visits, taking part in
> political protests. (Ward 1991:151)

As Monica McWilliams points out, the political identities of many Northern Irish women were thus 'born of the immediate experience of social injustice, rather than as a consequence of a pre-existing ideological belief' (McWilliams 1995:21). In the light of later divisions, it is important to note the emergence of these 'accidental activists'.

This 'armed patriarchy' – a term first coined by feminist activist Cathy Harkin to explain the interconnections between militarism and masculinism – was the immediate local background and complex political and social context to the emergence of a movement specifically devoted to women's rights (McWilliams 1995:15). There had been some early initiatives, outside of the specifically 'Civil Rights' movement which I have already outlined. In 1971, for example, a group of working-class women had protested against the decision of Margaret Thatcher, then Minister of Education, to stop free school milk for children over the age of seven. Marching, picketing and lobbying were the tactics employed, with the women on one occasion borrowing two cows from the Farmer's Union for a demonstration at the City Hall (Edgerton-Walker 1986:72). Despite winning the support of Belfast City Council, this campaign, focusing on the welfare of working-class families, was ultimately unsuccessful, and the introduction of internment distracted attention from such purely social issues. However, it is also worth noting that even this kind of family-based issue split on sectarian lines, viewed by many Protestants as a Catholic/nationalist protest because 'Catholics had larger families' – a pertinent reminder of the ways in which public opinion can be manipulated in a divided society.

Other women's activity centred around the two universities – women academics in Coleraine focused on the issue of domestic violence, and drew in women from local housing estates; in Queen's University Belfast, a weekend of films resulted in the formation of the Northern Ireland Women's Rights Movement (NIWRM). Established in 1975, the new organisation aimed 'to spread a consciousness of women's oppression and mobilise the greatest possible numbers of women on feminist issues' (NIWRM *Manifesto* 1975). An immediate focus for their campaigning activities was to call for the extension of the British Sexual Discrimination Act to Northern Ireland, and their Charter listed issues on which most feminists could agree – equal pay, childcare, education, etc. The members were a mixture of civil rights and trade-union activists, academics, students, women's aid, republicans, socialists and communists. Like most other women's organisations of the period, it was envisaged as a coalition or umbrella group. Numbers were small, with never more than twenty to fifty people involved at any one time, though the stack of paperwork from the period makes this difficult to believe. However, in a body which encompassed such a diversity of political allegiances and aspirations and which operated in the context of intense civil unrest, tensions were bound to surface. Some of the disagreements were all too familiar to the wider women's movement – with divisions amongst different brands of socialists, between radicals and reformists, and with those demanding women-only organisations. The Women's Aid movement, for example, disliked what they termed the bureaucratic nature of NIWRM, that it had a structure with a committee and a chairperson rather than a looser, more democratic grouping. Women's Aid was also said to be more overtly 'feminist' in nature. While any definition of feminism is always open to dispute, the distinction being made here was between those fighting to end women's oppression on a women-only basis, and those who were prepared to work with men to achieve female equality. Women's Aid belonged to the former grouping and it eventually withdrew from NIWRM after a heated debate over the involvement of men – the NIWRM actively lobbied trade unionists. However, the immediate local context further problematised the usual theoretical debates between feminists, with Women's Aid, for example, coming under heavy criticism from republican paramilitary groups for speaking out against their practice of tarring and feathering young women who fraternised with British soldiers (Roulston 1989:226).

It is difficult to separate specifically women's issues from broader campaigns for social justice in the region in these years. The various strands were often tightly interwoven, and many women themselves would not have seen them as distinct or separate issues. For many activists, for example, female inequality was only one consequence of

79

colonial oppression, while others, accepting the legitimacy of the state, saw no need to press for more than gender reform in the liberal tradition. Debates over the extension of British legislation to Northern Ireland involved broader consideration than one's position on abortion or employment law, and led to lengthy and heated exchanges. Demands that NIWRM support issues such as the 'troops out' campaign, or political status for republican prisoners were made in the context of an atmosphere of anger, fear and anxiety, when nightly news bulletins of the grieving relatives of victims of bombs and bullets dominated the television screen, and all aspects of life were affected by bomb scares, army searches and polarised communities. Women's views on these matters were determined by their religion, ethnicity, upbringing, education and where they lived. In the seventies it was not possible to be ambivalent. It's not surprising therefore that feminists in Northern Ireland faced real problems in identifying the oppressor and locating the source of oppression. We are familiar with issues around the term feminist itself, but the sensitivity to language and terminology in Northern Ireland goes much further, with many divergent views on what constitutes freedom, liberation or, indeed, peace. The name Northern Ireland is not acceptable to republicans who reject the legality of the province, and prefer to call it the six counties – just one example of the range of possible positionings in this complex situation. Support for women political prisoners, all of whom were republican, was a particularly emotive and divisive issue, which surfaced in the 1970s and would dominate much of the 1980s. These prisoners, like their male counterparts, took part in hunger strikes and, in 1979, in the dirty protest – with images of them wrapped in blankets, with matted, tangled hair and filthy skin in cells covered with human excrement – arousing both massive support and massive revulsion. Debates about their situation, argues Begona Aretxaga, were to spark 'a transformation of dominant discourses of feminism and nationalism' (Aretxaga 1995:47).

The NIWRM, concerned to maintain a broad-based women's movement, attempted to distance itself from the wider political and military struggle and declared itself to be non-aligned, though it did express opposition to emergency repressive legislation and condemned both paramilitary violence and the excessive use of violence by the security forces. When taken to task on their stance by nationalists, they argued that the ongoing IRA campaign was dividing the Protestant and Catholic communities more and more irrevocably, and rather than support them, the first task of the women's movement should be to work for the unity of the working class and between women. They argued that the women prisoners were simply aping the men, and that the republican movement was itself male dominated and patriarchal. They also defended themselves from accusations of complicity with the state:

> We have condemned the British army on many occasions ... we have decided to work for a women's movement independent of political parties and political positions. The refusal to take up positions on these general questions is not because we fear disunity and conflict: we believe that sticking to feminist issues is the best way to achieve feminist ends ... the fact that ... women prisoners are demanding political status does not make it a feminist issue any more than the fact that Cumann na mBan[1] exists makes a United Ireland a feminist aim.
>
> (Evason 1991:23)

They pointed out that no one proposed any alternatives to dealing with British legislation. Certainly the Republic of Ireland, dominated by the Catholic Church and deeply suppressive of women, was not viewed as an option. Though acknowledging that they were divided by differing priorities, the movement attempted to suppress them, obviously aware also of how these issues would appeal to or alienate the wider constituency of women in Northern Ireland.

Certainly the views of NIWRM were not acceptable to many feminists who viewed capitalism and imperialism as the major enemy. Those who aimed to combine their prior commitment to socialism with feminist and nationalist concerns formed the Socialist Women's Group in 1975, dissolving two years later with many members reuniting in the Belfast Women's Collective (Evason 1991:26). They argued that 'whilst the link with the British state remains, the working class will remain deeply divided', and that 'doctrines of ascendancy and dominance could not be reconciled with feminism' (Evason 1991:24-8). However, though they were anti-imperialist, this group was highly critical of the republican movement – particularly its position on women. Labelled as republican by the NIWRM because they were against the British presence, they were dismissed as a bourgeois women's group by others because of their criticism of republicanism. Their increasing political isolation, their consciousness of their own divergent views and the seemingly endless need to justify themselves to others, led to the group's dissolution in May 1980.

Women Against Imperialism (WAI) and the Relatives' Action Committee (RAC) provided forums for campaigns more closely linked with the rights of political prisoners. Women Against Imperialism emerged after a debate in the NIWRM over the Peace People in 1976.[2] This hugely popular movement was in fact given only a cautious welcome from the NIWRM, who claimed that it was a positive initiative, which provided a focus for people in despair. Others, however, felt that their political naïveté did more harm than good, and would not support the notion of peace at any price. Marie Mulholland argued:

> We wanted to have a woman's movement, and of course we wanted to be feminists and we wanted feminist social change. But we also had this war to deal with and we couldn't run away from that. (Miller et al 1996:18)

For WAI, the republican women prisoners were 'patriots . . . engaging in a separate struggle . . . even to the point of death', and deserved the whole-hearted support of all Irish women. In a letter to the *Irish Times*, the prisoners themselves suggested that the NIWRM needed to consider their definition of feminism: they argued that the prisoners' issue was

> a feminist issue in so far as we are women, and the network of this jail is completely geared to male domination . . . we are subject to physical and mental abuse from male guards who patrol our wing daily, continually peeping into our cells. . . . If this is not a feminist issue then we feel that the word feminist needs to be redefined.
> (No Wash Protestors August 1980)

Women's Aid responded with a call for a prisoners' rights organisation, but argued that 'the struggle for political status was best left to the political organisations involved'; they noted, however, that the resulting brutalisation of the whole prison system could not be overlooked (Derry Women's Aid 1980:14). The NIWRM expressed anxiety about how the situation in Northern Ireland was affecting feminism and its growth. Following the 1979 International Women's Day protests outside Armagh prison they announced:

> we have been worried by reports reaching us from Britain, about the position British feminists appear to be taking in relation to Ireland. We think that many of these have been taken as a result of the recent visit to Ireland of British feminists on International Women's Day. . . . we are worried that many of them have gone on from that visit to substitute emotionalism and guilt-tripping for feminist thought and action. (NIWRM 1980:15)

Alarm was expressed about apparently uncritical support of nationalism and republicanism. One woman explained her position on the prisoners:

> It is hard to separate out the strands of their struggle. I
> can support their struggle as women fighting their
> repressive conditions, like lack of sanitary conditions, their
> lack of educational facilities, lack of childcare and medical
> care, but I do not feel that the movement for which they
> are in prison cares much about them as WOMEN – only
> as republicans. (Gerry 1980:30-33)

Outside Women Against Imperialism, the Relatives' Action Committee and the broader republican movement, the view was prevalent that male republicans were using women prisoners and their supporters as pawns in the ongoing political struggle. As the NIWRM pointed out, the IRA frequently engaged in or encouraged the tarring and feathering or other forms of paramilitary violence against women who offended them in their tightly-controlled neighborhoods. Gender continued to define power relations both inside and outside the prison walls.

One lesbian, who asserted that as a 'radical feminist I do not support the Republican movement', claimed that the only analysis heard in the south of Ireland or Britain was the republican one: 'From women in this movement I have met with the assumption that if you oppose women's involvement in republican politics it must be because you are a Protestant, pro-British reactionary' (Allen 1980).

Commentators have frequently noted that nationalists and republicans dominated the women's movement in the north. It is certainly true that those who came from a tradition that was vehemently opposed to the political establishment would have found in radical feminism a more coherent political agenda. Similarly:

> the historical accommodation between republicanism and
> feminism, and the links between feminism and opposition
> or liberation politics also pose a challenge to unionist
> ideology. (Rooney 1995:44)

This did not mean, however, that Protestant women were not involved. Indeed, Lynda Edgerton, chair of the NIWRM in its early years, was clear that the movement included women from both sides of the religious divide. She argues that the fact that many Protestant feminist activists were also members of the Communist party, together with lack of documentation of their experiences, means they are often overlooked (McWilliams 1995:35). Discussions with Protestant women who remained outside the broad women's movement, however, suggest that the perception of that movement was that it was nationalist and Catholic and firmly linked to the Civil Rights movement. May Blood (now

Baroness Blood), an active woman trade unionist in the 1970s, recalled it in these terms, adding that on the Shankill Road where she lived it was also regarded as full of 'butch lesbians' (Interview with the author, April 2002). The term was meant to convey an image of femininity unacceptable to the 'respectable' Protestant Unionist community. The explanation for these diverging views on Protestant participation is, of course, that Protestantism and Unionism are not synonymous, but that Protestants involved with any kind of anti-state grouping would have been viewed as 'green Protestants', disloyal and engaged in the betrayal of a country which was under threat. As Eilish Rooney points out:

> a debate over female identity within unionism or the pos-
> sibility of unionism accommodating any form of feminism
> did not take place until the early 1990s. (Rooney 1995:42)

In an interview with Rosemary Sales, 'Julie', brought up in Protestant East Belfast, explained why she found the women's movement alienating:

> I went to a Protestant church school, I was brought up
> with that culture. Our perceptions were different. In the
> women's movement it was not possible to express it. The
> only experience that was valued was of the down-trodden
> Catholic woman. (Sales 1998:153)

Fermanagh woman Ruth Moore, discussing the need to 'transcend sectarianism and the imposition of a one-size-fits-all identity', described how as a Protestant woman she experienced her identity as other to English women and the British state, other to Catholic women and Catholic domination in Ireland as a whole, and other to Protestant men in Northern Ireland (Moore 1994:6). Moreover, once the conflict was underway, with religion, however simplistically, seen as determining national aspirations, it became increasingly difficult for more liberal Protestants to openly associate with those perceived to be Catholic/ nationalist/republican. The sectarian nature of the conflict limited co-operation across the boundaries of segregated communities. In addition to these divisions, there were real practical problems around getting women organised:

> how do you expect us to leave our homes if our son is
> going to be, at best lifted (by army/police) or at worst
> shot dead by the time we get back? (NIWRM 1980)

No wonder that one activist from the period later described the seventies women's movement as 'invigorating, exasperating and demoralising';

'a wheel with spokes and a rim but no centre' (Evason 1991:57).

The complexity and controversy surrounding the whole nature of the relationships between individuals and the state in Northern Ireland ensured that the struggle there was of a particularly painful nature. Feminism in the north of Ireland represented only one strand in a wider struggle affecting political, social and personal life, and women prioritised different aspects of their identities in different ways at different times and, as one former activist admitted, 'we failed to talk about our divisions in a manner which makes us face them and not deny them' (Miller et al 1996:18).

But the emphasis on division, failure and negation ignores what was accomplished as a result of feminist activity. The formation of Women's Aid and the setting up of Rape Crisis Centres were important achievements, as was the work of the Law and Research Group, and the influential publications of NIWRM – on contract cleaning, hairdressing and gender divisions in education. Persistent lobbying helped push forward legislation for equal pay: an act was passed in 1970 and this was followed by a Sex Discrimination Act in 1976. The profile of International Women's Day was greatly raised almost single-handedly by Lynda Edgerton. In 1978, feminists throughout Northern Ireland came together to secure the release of Noreen Winchester, imprisoned for killing the father who had raped and abused her. When I asked Lynda about the most important achievement of the movement, she had no hesitation – the opening of the first Women's Advice Centre in Belfast in 1979. May Blood agreed; indeed it is widely accepted that the opening of women's centres has been one of the most critical moves in the politicisation of Northern Irish women, ensuring their involvement in mainstream social and economic issues. A Trades Council paper written in the 1980s claimed:

> the women's movement has helped to redefine the baseline in politics and has made an important contribution to the modernization of Irish politics and has contributed to creating a climate conducive to the development of progressive and women's class politics.
>
> (Belfast Trades Council 1987)

Nonetheless, and perhaps not surprisingly given the focus on militarism and constitutional politics historically, women in mainstream histories and analyses have been 'denied, stereotyped or marginalized' (Bell 1998:216). It has been acknowledged by many commentators that women were the 'backbone of their communities' during the conflict – an image which conjures up the stereotype of strong mothers protecting and defending the home. In most analyses, however, they are portrayed as 'passive victims of the troubles, viragos of the barricades, or advocates of a messianic peace' (Rolston 1989:56). In addition, much feminist analysis on Northern Ireland has been specifically concerned with post-colonialism, with the links between nationalism and feminism, and with the 'embodiment' of protest and of suffering – women prisoners. As Bill Rolston points out, none of these stereotypes reveal the true situation of women living in a socially deprived, war-torn, rigidly patriarchal society' (Rolston 1989:56).

There are thus several conceptual and practical problems with the discussion of women's equality in many areas of life in Northern Ireland, when as we have seen people were positioned differently in different discourses (Francis 2002:46). Ideas of collectivity are only possible when other differences are suppressed. Nor is it possible to simply add on different aspects of identity to that of gender: for example, the women who came into the women's movement through their experience of conflict with the state – the 'accidental activists' discussed earlier – had their feminism shaped by that experience. It proved impossible for them to create a sisterhood with those for whom that same state was upheld as a bulwark against the Catholicism of the Republic, the violence of the IRA, link to British heritage, or whatever . . . Our gendered identity is thus only one factor shaping the realities of our lives and making us the type of women we are. These other differences have important effects on the similarities between women. Cynthia Cockburn maintained that while both Catholic and Protestant working-class communities in Northern Ireland suffer poverty, violence and political neglect, women in these communities experience these things in distinctive, gendered ways (Cockburn 1998:53). However, gender is not the only category of identity that holds consequences for people's life outcomes; there is a difference in the status and power of some women over other women. Referring to women's inclusions in and admissions to, or exclusions from party politics (or socio-economic and cultural influence), Eilish Rooney argues that these

> are not *the same* for Catholic women as they are for Prot-
> estant women. They are not the same for working-class
> republican women as for middle-class nationalist women;
> for working-class loyalist women as for middle-class
> unionist women. (Rooney 2000:166)

That there was no consensus on the meaning of 'feminism' and the agenda for a women's movement during the 1970s is not so surprising now, when attempts to define feminism are resisted and it is asserted that women are an incoherent and unstable category. And we would expect conflict to be inherent in any movement attempting to represent the interests of lives 'lived within the ideological constructs and political structures of religion, nationalism, race, class, and history' (Rooney 1995:44). The lessons of the period have been painfully learned. And we could argue that important initiatives today have only been possible because of that experience, of having to work through difficult issues, and that the legacy of the seventies remains critical to the ongoing debates on conflict resolution in Northern Ireland.

In 2002 no one claims that there is one feminist agenda. But there is evidence of what Yuval-Davis calls 'a mode of coalition politics in which the differential positionings of the individuals and collectives involved . . . [are] recognized as well as the value systems which underlie their struggles' (Yuval-Davis 1997:25). At least some of these can be traced back to the long-term impact of seventies movements and, indeed, many of the same individual women are involved. The most quoted example in Ireland is that of the Northern Ireland Women's Coalition, putting religious differences aside and offering an alternative agenda to mainstream politics in Northern Ireland (Fearon 1999). That coalition itself came out of grassroots women's community activism, in which, while many women involved are not feminist, there are often feminist principles being put into action at leadership level. In groups across Northern Ireland women are not only active within their own communities, but on some occasions also maintain alliances across traditional divides. The Women's Support Network in Belfast, for example, has been cited as a space where agreement for action can be negotiated. Feminism has also now impacted on other categories of identity. The growing importance of the women's sector within Sinn Fein and the republican movement, from the early 1980s, can be traced to pressures from groups such as WAI and the RAC, and to the high profile given to republican women prisoners. Within Unionism too, it has been recognised at both party political and grassroots community levels that women need to articulate their own demands, and express their identity. Of course these changes have themselves taken place in a changing context – most importantly the peace process, which has provided space for reflection on strategies, actions and alliances. The nature of Irish nationalism has also changed, while the Irish Republic is slowly moving away from its dominant Catholic ethos.

The diversity of the women's movement in Northern Ireland was by no means unique, but was common to left-wing movements of all kinds and in all countries. It provides a particularly difficult and emotive reminder of the multiple identities and conflicting loyalties held by women everywhere. As Audre Lorde so succinctly put it:

> the strength of the women's movement will not be found in a measure of how it can set aside differences to better work together, but in how it can harness the energy of those differences and provide a working example of how to deal with them. (Lorde in Bell 1998:230)

Notes

1 Cumann na mBan, originally founded in 1913 before the Easter Rising to support the Irish Volunteers, was the female auxiliary of the IRA, and operated mainly in a supportive role to the military.

2 The Peace People was the name given to an organisation formed in August 1976 after three children were killed by a car which ran out of control in the aftermath of a shooting incident. Mairead Corrigan, the children's aunt, and Betty Williams channelled the resulting anger and emotion into a campaign of mass marches and demonstrations, and were awarded the Nobel Peace Prize in 1977.

Bibliography

Allen, Pat (March, 1980) 'We must not be content with any secondhand analysis with its roots in male power politics', reprinted in *Scarlet Women II: Newsletter of the Socialist Feminist Current of the Women's Liberation Movement* Belfast.

Aretxaga, Begona (1995) 'Dirty Protest: Symbolic Overdetermination and Gender in Northern Ireland Ethnic Violence', *Ethos* 23, 2:123-48.

Belfast Trades Council (1987) 'Northern Ireland Women's Rights Movement', unpublished paper in NIWRM archives. Linenhall Library Belfast.

Bell, Christine (1998) 'Women, Equality and Political Participation', in J. Anderson and J. Goodman (eds) *DIS/Agreeing Ireland: Contexts, Obstacles, Hopes* London: Pluto.

Cockburn, Cynthia (1998) *The Space Between Us: Negotiating Gender and National Identities in Conflict* London: Zed.

Derry Women's Aid (1980) Press Statement on Armagh Prison, reprinted in *Scarlet Women II: Newsletter of the Socialist Feminist Current of the Women's Liberation Movement* Belfast:14.

Edgerton-Walker, Lynda (1986) 'Public Protest, Domestic Acquiescence: Women in Northern Ireland', in Rosemary Ridd and Helen Callaway (eds) *Caught up in Conflict: Women's Responses to Political Strife* London: MacMillan Education in association with Oxford University.

Evason, Eileen (1991) *Against the Grain: The Contemporary Women's Movement in Northern Ireland* Dublin: Attic Press.

Fearon, Kate (1999) *Women's Work: The Story of the Northern Ireland Women's Coalition* Belfast: Blackstaff Press.

Feldman, Allen (1991) *Formations of Violence: The Narrative of the Body and Political Terror in Northern Ireland* Chicago: University of Chicago Press.

Francis, Becky (2002) 'Relativism, Realism, and Feminism: an analysis of some theoretical tensions in research on gender identity', *Journal of Gender Studies* 11, 1:39-54.

Gerry (1980) 'Notes on Feminism and Northern Ireland', reprinted in *Scarlet Women II: Newsletter of the Socialist Feminist Current of the Women's Liberation Movement* Belfast.

McKay, Susan (2000) *Northern Protestants: An Unsettled People* Belfast: Blackstaff Press.

McWilliams, Monica (1995) 'Struggling for Peace and Justice: Reflections on Women's Activism in Northern Ireland', in Joan Hoff and Maureen Coulter (eds) *Irish Women's Voices: Past and Present* Indiana: Journal of Women's History.

Miller, Robert Lee, Rick Wilford and Fred Donaghue (1996) *Women and Political Participation in Northern Ireland* Aldershot: Avebury.

Moore, Ruth (June/July 1994) 'Proper Wives, Orange Maidens or Disloyal Subjects: Situating the Equality Concern of Protestant Women in Northern Ireland', *Women's News*:69.

NIWRM (1975) *Manifesto*, NIWR archives.

NIWRM (1980) 'Northern Ireland 5 Years On', NIWR archives.

No Wash Protestors (1980) *Irish Times* August.

O'Connor, Fionnuala (1993) *In Search of a State: Catholics in Northern Ireland* Belfast: Blackstaff Press.

Rolston, Bill (1989) 'Mothers, whores and villains: images of women in novels of the Northern Ireland conflict', *Race & Class* 31, 1:41-57.

Rooney, Eilish (1995) 'Political Division, Practical Alliance: Problems for Women in Conflict', in Joan Hoff and Maureen Coulter (eds) I*rish Women's Voices: Past and Present* Indiana: Journal of Women's History.

Rooney, Eilish (2000) 'Women in Northern Irish Politics: Difference Matters', in Carmel Roulston and Celia Davies (eds) *Gender, Democracy and Inclusion in Northern Ireland* Basingstoke: MacMillan.

Roulston, Carmel (1989) 'Women on the Margin: The Women's Movement in Northern Ireland, 1973-1988', *Science & Society* 53, 2:219-36.

Sales, Rosemary (1998) 'Women, the Peace Makers?', in James Anderson and James Goodman (eds) *DIS/Agreeing Ireland: Contexts, Obstacles, Hope* London: Pluto.

Shannon, Catherine (1995) 'Women in Northern Ireland', in Mary O'Dowd and Sabine Wichert (eds) *Chattel, Servant or Citizen: Women's Status in Church, State and Society* Belfast: Institute of Irish Studies.

Sinn Fein Women's Department (1991) *Women in Struggle* Spring:1.

Ward, Margaret (1991) 'The Women's Movement in the North of Ireland', in Sean Hutton and Paul Stewart (eds) *Ireland's Histories: Aspects of State, Society and Ideology* London: Routledge.

Yuval-Davis, Nira (1997) 'Women, ethnicity and empowerment: Towards transversal politics', *Gender and Nation* London: Sage.

A Piece of the Seventies:
Reading Michèle Roberts' *A Piece of the Night*

Julie Palmer

A Piece of the Night tells the story of Julie Fanchot: from her
early relationships with men, to her first lesbian relationship; her marriage to Ben, her struggles to negotiate her
relationship with her mother; her difficulties adapting to the
conventional feminine role and her dialogue with feminism.

Michèle Roberts' earliest novel, *A Piece of the Night*, was published in
1978, when I was two years old. I first picked it up in 2002 when it was
republished by The Women's Press as a 'classic'. I read it for pleasure and
then returned to it once more, fascinated by the novelist's engagement
with feminist issues.

A Piece of the Night is a product of the Feminist Seventies, yet as I was
writing this piece I began to think about what dates the work. Perhaps
Julie's clothes: her 'felt skirt dotted with patches, beads and bits of rib-
bon', worn with clogs (2002:23) or her silver dungarees. Or the sight of
a procession celebrating International Labour Day: Socialists and Feminists marching on the streets of Oxford. Or Julie's lifestyle: the household Ben calls 'his experimental commune'.

Despite such hallmarks of the Feminist Seventies, I find it quite hard to
locate the novel in 'the seventies'. To me, *A Piece of the Night* has continuing relevance as feminist fiction (as well as simply being a good
read) and the interaction between reader and text creates a dialogue in
the here and now. So many themes of the book remain pertinent - the
mother-daughter relationship, gender roles, female sexuality, attitudes
to the female body. It would be wonderful to be able to read this novel
as a piece of history, and I am reminded of Zöe Fairbairns' answer, at the
Feminist Seventies Conference, to the question 'when will you know
you've won?' Her reply was: when the demands of the WLM 'look as
old-fashioned as campaigning for the right to vote'. Sadly, the contem-

julie palmer

porary reader can still recognise and identify with many of the novel's topics: the taboos around menstruation, the power imbalance in heterosexual relationships and sexual coercion, the hostility lesbian women often encounter, the ideology of romantic love fed to young women and the concomitant disillusionment with the reality of relationships, the quest for thinness and beauty, the pressures to inscribe (hetero) sexualised femininity on the surface of her body.

This is not to say that feminism has not achieved anything in the last twenty-something years, only that there is more to be gained. The WLM has a past and a future and a reader might engage with this 'piece' of the feminist seventies in any number of ways - she may read it as a historical artefact or she may find herself using it as a way of thinking about contemporary women and their lives. She will not be disappointed.

92

Bibliography

Roberts, Michèle [1978](2002) *A Piece of the Night* London: The Women's Press Ltd.

Saying What We Want:

Women's Liberation and the Seven Demands

Zoë Fairbairns

In her poem 'The Old Feminist', the US poet

Phyllis McGinley (who died in 1978) pokes fun at the ageing activist who, after a lifetime of heady campaigning and some successes:

> ... Takes no pleasure in her rights
> Who so enjoyed her wrongs.[1]

I don't want to be like her, so I must try not to wallow too much in nostalgia as I look back through my rose-tinted spectacles at the Feminist Seventies – the good old days when everything was terrible.

The truth is that neither I nor anybody else 'enjoys her wrongs' while she is actually suffering them. But years later it may be possible to enjoy those wrongs in retrospect – particularly when some of those wrongs have been righted, and particularly if you were part of a political movement that can take some credit for bringing this about.

In this article, based on a talk I gave at The Feminist Seventies Conference, I look at one of seventies feminism's most characteristic and successful tactics: making demands.

For me, the Feminist Seventies began in late 1969, which was when I first encountered the words 'women's', 'liberation' and 'movement' side by side in the same phrase.

I was studying in the USA at the time, and my immediate thought was, why haven't we got something like this at home? By the time I returned to the UK in the summer of 1970, Women's Liberation (WL) was already establishing itself, not simply as an offshoot of the US movement, but as a home-grown response to home-grown sexual politics.

I found that there had been a conference held in Oxford in February 1970, at which the burgeoning Women's Liberation Movement (WLM) had agreed to campaign for four demands.

These were:

(1) Equal pay for equal work
(2) Equal education and equal opportunities
(3) Free contraception and abortion on demand
(4) Free 24 hour nurseries.

I thought these demands were brilliant, striking at the very heart of why and how women were oppressed.

The main cause of women's oppression – it seemed to me – was that women tended to get married, have children and so become financially dependent on men and under their control. This was so obviously a bad arrangement for women that we must only be doing it because we had to. We were forced into it, I thought, by a lack of other options. If, however, demands (1) and (2) were met, women would be able to get good jobs and live independently. If demand (3) were met, we wouldn't have to have babies, and if demand (4) were met, even if we did have babies, we would be able to take paid work as well and so avoid coming under male financial control. QED, problem of patriarchy solved.

Another benefit that I thought would come out of giving women a real choice of whether to marry, and/or have sex with men, and/or have babies, was that those heterosexual men who refused to mend their patriarchal ways would soon find it impossible to get a mate. They would thus be deprived of the joys of female sexual companionship, which in many cases would be enough to bring them into line. Alternatively, their genes would die out. Either way, that would be the end of patriarchy. This desirable state of affairs would, in my view, be further hastened by the achievement of three more demands which were added at subsequent conferences[2] in the Feminist Seventies. These were:

(5) Legal and financial independence for women
(6) An end to discrimination against lesbians
(7) Freedom for all women from intimidation by the threat or use of male violence. An end to the laws, assumptions and institutions that perpetuate male dominance and men's aggression towards women.

That should just about fix it, I thought.

You might think I was a bit naïve, and I might even agree with you. But you don't have to see the Seven Demands as an answer to all women's problems, either in the Feminist Seventies or now, to recognise the advantages of saying what you want.

The first and most obvious advantage is that it is better than the alternative, ie not saying what you want. Saying that you want something – demanding it – does not necessarily mean that you will get it, but not saying what you want more or less guarantees that you will not get it. And even if you do, you may not recognise it.

Before you can say what you want, you have to know what that is. You have to think about it, discuss it, agree on it. You have to ask yourself what, in specific terms, is standing between the way things are now and the way you would like them to be. Is it a law, a tradition, an economic structure or system (local, national, global or domestic), an ideology, a personal grievance, all or none of the above? Is it bigger than that, or smaller? You don't necessarily have to have all the answers, but you have to know what you think, you have to be specific, and you have to prioritise. You have to risk unpopularity by saying, 'this, not that' or 'this now, that later.' Those of us who were not at the 1970 conference owe a huge debt to those who were, and who dared to do these things.

Another advantage of having a list of clear demands was that it provided an answer to the frequently asked question, 'What do feminists want?' Or, as a man once put it to me, 'How will you know when you've won?' I showed him a list of the demands and said, 'I'll know we've won when each of those demands has been met, and when they look as old-fashioned as campaigning for the right to vote.'

Has that day come? Hardly. But significant progress was made, during the Feminist Seventies and subsequently, towards the achievement of most of the demands, and much of that was as a result of feminist campaigning in its broadest sense.

Here are a few examples.

First demand: Equal pay. Women in 1970 earned only 66 percent of what men earned. Now the figure is 83 percent. That's still not equal pay, but these days at least some of the discrepancy is due to women doing different jobs from men, and following different working patterns. To some extent this reflects women's different choices and priorities, which makes it a different sort of problem (and in my opinion a lesser one) from the pre-1970s practice of employers openly and unashamedly offering men and women different rates for doing the same job. That is now illegal. Similarly, the old trade union ideal of the 'family wage' (ie more money for men because they have to support a family, less money for women because they have men to support them) is rarely advocated these days, at least in public.

Second demand: Equal opportunities. When the Equal Pay Act was passed in 1970, many employers responded by segregating men and women into different jobs so that they would have no basis for comparison. But in 1975 the Sex Discrimination Act made this illegal, along with the practice of offering jobs to only one sex. This was quite normal before the Feminist Seventies, with newspapers running job advertisements in separate columns for men and women, and Labour Exchanges (government-run predecessors of Job Centres) displaying men's jobs and women's jobs in different windows.

Third demand: Contraception and abortion. The only time that I have ever consulted a doctor as a private patient was in 1969 when I wanted to go on the pill. The doctor in question was my NHS GP, who informed me that although he had no objection to giving me the pill, he was not legally permitted to do it on the National Health. So I had to pay a fee to see him, and the full cost of the medication on a private prescription – and very posh it was too, with twirly writing. The cost was two or three times the normal prescription fee. Another alternative would have been to go to a Family Planning Association clinic or a Brook Advisory Centre, but although both these bodies were charities and doing great work, you still had to pay. Since 1975, however, anyone who needs contraceptive advice or supplies can get them free on the National Health.

Abortion, although neither free nor on demand for everyone, is widely available. Attempts by anti-abortionists to restrict it were robustly and successfully resisted in the Feminist Seventies by the feminist-inspired National Abortion Campaign (NAC) and A Woman's Right To Choose.

Fourth demand: Childcare. In 1970, just 10 percent of children under the age of five had a state-funded nursery place. The present government has guaranteed a nursery place for every four-year-old whose parents want it, and in its National Childcare Strategy acknowledges the importance of childcare for education, equal opportunities and social inclusion. That's still a long way from free twenty-four hour childcare for all, and, like all government promises, it needs to be watched. But at least now there is something to watch.

Fifth demand: Legal and financial independence. In the early 1970s, many laws, official regulations and commercial practices took it for granted that women were financially dependent on men, thus ensuring that this dependency, where it existed, was difficult to escape from. It was, for example, normal practice for income tax returns to bear the words, 'If you are a married woman, this form should be given to your husband and treated as if it were addressed to him'; a wife's tax affairs were her husband's responsibility. Tax rebates owed to wives were frequently paid to their husbands, and it was not uncommon, if a married woman wrote to the Inland Revenue about some matter to do with her income tax, for the reply to come back to her husband, beginning, 'Dear Sir, with reference to your wife's letter, the answer to her question is . . . '

Many social security benefits were payable to women at a lower rate than to men, or not payable to women at all. (Invalid Care Allowance, a payment for people who gave up paid work to look after someone who was ill, was only payable to men and single women. Married women were deemed not to need it, because they would be at home anyway.)

Almost all family benefits were paid to the 'head of the household', which, unless he was actually incapacitated, meant the man. All this has now changed, thanks in part to the energetic and well-informed lobbying of the Women's Liberation Campaign for Legal and Financial Independence, later renamed 'The Fifth Demand'.

Women's Liberation groups were also active in the 1970s in defending Family Allowance (later renamed Child Benefit) which was the only independent income received by many mothers. Governments of both main parties (Edward Heath's Tories in 1971-2 and James Callaghan's Labour Party in 1976) tried to change this and pay the benefit to breadwinners, which usually meant fathers; but on both occasions, feminist-led public outrage was so strongly in favour of the payment going to mothers, that plans to change this were abandoned.

Another problem related to consumer credit. It was common practice for shops and financial institutions to require a woman who wanted to borrow money – anything from an HP agreement to replace a toaster, to a mortgage to buy a house – to have the form countersigned by her husband or another man, to guarantee the payment. Even if she was in a well-paid job, she was assumed to be unreliable. This practice was outlawed in the Consumer Credit Act of 1974.

Sixth demand: Discrimination against lesbians. Unlike male homosexuality, lesbianism has never been illegal in the UK. But in the past there was much less social acceptance of lesbianism than there is now, when even cabinet ministers feel free to come out, and popular soap operas seem incomplete without a lesbian storyline. It is now much easier for lesbian couples to live openly, have fertility treatments, foster and adopt children, and own property together. But lesbian couples (like gay men) are still treated less favourably than married couples in terms of tax, inheritance and some employment rights; and Clause 28 of the 1988 Local Government Act, which restricts free speech on all forms of homosexuality, means that in some ways lesbians are now more disadvantaged than they were in the 1970s.

Seventh demand: Patriarchal violence, institutions and attitudes. It's difficult to comment briefly on this huge and wide ranging demand. Male violence to women is still a horrendous problem; the fact that there are now refuges and crisis lines (many of which had their origins in the Feminist Seventies) is some consolation, but not much. Still, it is true to say that many patriarchal attitudes which were taken for granted before the seventies, are now widely condemned. One such was the notion that a married woman was her husband's property, and that by marrying him she had relinquished her right to refuse sex. This was the legal position in the Feminist Seventies – indeed, it did not change until 1992, which was when it first became possible under English law for a married woman whose husband had sex with her against her will, to charge him with rape.

Other attitudes which were once widespread but are now far less common are the assumption that women's chastity is more important than men's; that married women should not go out to work; that a woman who is sexually harassed in the workplace should keep quiet and look for another job; that single motherhood is a matter for shame and disgrace; and that the title 'Ms' will never catch on.

In listing these partial successes of the Seven Demands, I am not saying that they solved everything, or that they represented the only feminist political activity at the time, or that all feminists agreed with them. But they were widely accepted, and provided an important way of presenting the WLM to the rest of the world.

The way they did this provides, I think, a potted history of some aspects of the Feminist Seventies.

By the middle of the decade, there was huge interest in the WLM, with enquiries pouring into women's centres. I was a paid worker at one of these centres (the Women's Research and Resources Centre – WRRC) from 1975 to 1977, and continued my involvement as a volunteer into the eighties.

Letters came from students writing essays, school students doing projects, journalists, politicians, or members of the public who had been intrigued or fired up by something they had seen in a newspaper or heard on the radio. Sometimes we didn't know what lay behind the enquiries, when they just said things like, 'Dear Sir, I am doing research on women, please send details'. What they all seemed to be asking, in their different ways, was, 'What is women's liberation? What is it for, what is it against, what does it do and where can I find it?'

The strictly correct response, of course, in a determinedly non-centralised movement, would have been to mutter, 'It's not for me to say' or 'Well, here's what I think, but I'm not the spokeswoman or anything, I'm certainly not the leader, so if you really want to know you'll have to ask everybody else . . . ' by which time most of the enquirers would have lost patience and gone away.

So the WRRC got together with two other women's centres - A Woman's Place, and the Women's Information, Referral and Education Service (WIRES) – to produce a leaflet that would explain the WLM in a way that we would all be happy to endorse and send to our enquirers.

The leaflet was called *Women's Liberation – An Introduction*. Producing the first edition was one of the shortest, easiest feminist tasks I have ever been involved with. So far as I remember, we didn't even meet. We didn't have to. We did it all either over the phone or by sending drafts through the post (no email in those days). We simply used the demands – the agreed programme of the WLM – as the basis of our introduction. We listed the demands, explained what they meant and why they were important, gave the names and addresses of groups campaigning around the issues and added some suggestions for further reading. We printed 10,000 copies and sent them out to enquirers, free of charge. Other feminist groups asked for copies for their own use; we either gave them away or sold them at cost. The first print run disappeared within weeks, and soon we were reprinting.

As the demands were added to, the leaflet needed to be modified. Once again, the WRRC, A Woman's Place and WIRES took on the task. This time there was a little bit more discussion, but not much. I think we met once, maybe twice. Lesbians in the group felt that the section on lesbian rights should be written by lesbians. Everyone agreed. Someone else wanted to include sections on consciousness raising and the small-groups structure of the WLM. Again, no controversy there. Addresses and reading lists were updated, and cartoons were added.[3] Again, many thousands of copies were printed, sold, given away or mailed out to enquirers.

In 1978, at the Birmingham WL conference, the demands were changed once again. (The final text appears at the end of this article.) Once again, *Women's Liberation – An Introduction* was out of date. So did we meet again to update it?

Not at once. For one thing, there were still plenty of copies of the 1977 edition left over, and for another, voices were being raised criticising the demands as too reformist, tinkering with oppressive structures rather than overthrowing them. And the WLM was by now so bitterly divided over issues including race, class and sexuality that the women who had produced the earlier versions of the leaflet no longer felt confident that we could, in a single document, do justice to all the competing views and provide an introduction to the WLM that would be fair, accurate and above all useful to outsiders.

For several years we dodged the issue, relying on earlier editions of the leaflet, or responding to the 'I am interested in women, please send details' enquiries with individual letters – well aware that these were even less democratic and representative than a cobbled together new edition of *Women's Liberation – An Introduction* would have been. Finally, in 1983, a group was formed within the Feminist Library (formerly the WRRC) to attempt the task.

We met a few times, but we couldn't get beyond the first page. The mere mention of the phrase 'equal pay' was enough to bring about radical challenges: why do we want to be equal with men, don't we want something better? What's the point of trying to improve the conditions of women in waged labour when we want to end the whole concept of waged labour by overthrowing capitalism? Dealing with other demands on the list was no easier. Discussions of contraception and abortion soon raised questions about whether women should be having penetrative sex with men in the first place, and whether, by trying to make it easier to avoid unwanted pregnancy, we were not simply encouraging male sexual irresponsibility. Talk of nurseries was seen in some quarters as implying criticism of women who wanted to look after their children themselves, the phrase 'legal and financial independence' was seen as both too individualistic and too close to wages for housework, and 'an end to discrimination against lesbians' was seen as much too modest a demand.

All these debates were important, but they didn't get the leaflet written. Soon the project was abandoned. As far as I know the leaflet has never been updated or reprinted, and neither, since 1978, has any Women's Liberation conference amended the demands, or added to them.

So was this the demise of the Seven Demands? Not quite. It was a feature of the structurelessness and ultra-democracy of seventies feminism that no decision or policy could ever be enforced on the WLM as a whole. But by the same token, it could not be repealed either, and this applies to the Seven Demands. They continued to exist well into the 1980s as a defining mark of what feminism meant for a substantial number of women.

For example, WIRES, which was the nearest thing the WLM ever had to a national newsletter, used them as editorial criteria. WIRES' policy was to publish, unedited, any contribution that was written by a woman, and did not contravene the Seven Demands. These rules made it easier for them to decide what to include – it meant, for example, that long debates about Northern Ireland or Palestine were included (they may not have had any direct connection with the Seven Demands, except perhaps the last one which covered everything, but they didn't actually contravene them); while contributions from a group called Feminists Against Abortion (who took the view that abortion was an abuse of women's bodies and right to bear children) were excluded as being in contravention of the third demand. With hindsight one might take different views on either of these points, but the women running WIRES had to have some sort of fixed and agreed editorial criteria. The Seven Demands provided these until WIRES folded in 1986.

The Seven Demands were also listed in the *Spare Rib Diary* (which provided an annually updated list of feminist groups, businesses and projects, and so was essential to any activist); and as recently as 2001, they appeared on the wall of the Silver Moon women's bookshop in London.

Silver Moon as an autonomous feminist bookshop no longer exists (though it has recently reopened as a shop-within-a-shop at Foyles[4]). *Spare Rib* and its diary are no more. No-one organises WL marches any longer like the one held in 1971 when women marched behind banners proclaiming their favourite demand; and I am not aware of any attempts to republish *Women's Liberation – An Introduction*. Nor have there been in recent years the sorts of WL conferences at which policy can be more-or-less made and more-or-less agreed on by more-or-less everybody. Maybe it was easier to do things like that when we felt more beleaguered, when our ideas seemed wacky and revolutionary, rather than mainstream and obvious as many of them do now. Maybe things were easier when they were more difficult.

I believe that the Seven Demands served a useful purpose by providing a minimum programme, a rallying point, a loose but sustaining structure for an otherwise-unstructured movement. They also provided a reminder of what it meant to call yourself a feminist, as opposed to the equally honourable but very different identifications of 'socialist who happens to be a woman', 'peace campaigner who happens to be a woman', 'ecological activist who happens to be a woman' and so on.

If the word 'feminist' has any meaning, it has to incorporate a belief that there is such a thing as sexual politics, a power struggle between men as men and women as women. The Seven Demands identified the points of political friction and conflict, and possible directions for feminist political creativity. They are certainly not reformist. If you think they are, take another look at them and try to imagine a world – or even just a small part of the world – in which they have all been fulfilled. Would it be a world that you would recognise? Or would it be one in which a revolution had occurred?

The Seven Demands

as finalised at the National Women's Liberation Conference held in Birmingham in 1978.

'The women's liberation movement asserts a woman's right to define her own sexuality, and demands:

1 Equal pay for equal work.
2 Equal education and job opportunities.
3 Free contraception and abortion on demand.
4 Free 24-hour community-controlled childcare.
5 Legal and financial independence for women.
6 An end to discrimination against lesbians.
7 Freedom for all women from intimidation by the threat or use of male violence. An end to the laws, assumptions and institutions which perpetuate male dominance and men's aggression towards women.'

Notes

1 These lines are quoted from childhood memory. Every effort has been made to locate the poem and to obtain copyright, but this has so far been unsuccessful.

2 Demands 5 and 6 were added at the Manchester conference in 1975; the 7th demand, and an overall introductory assertion – 'The women's liberation movement asserts a woman's right to define her own sexuality' – was added at the Birmingham conference in 1978.

3 Photocopies of the 1977 edition of *Women's Liberation – An Introduction,* can be obtained from me at: 27 Anerley Grove, London SE19 2HS. The print quality is not brilliant, but most of the text is legible. Please send three first class stamps to cover photocopying costs, and an A4 stamped addressed envelope.

4 To contact Silver Moon at Foyles: silvermoon@foyles.co.uk; 113-119 Charing Cross Road, London WC2H 0EB, England; +44(0)20 7437 5660. <http://foyles.co.uk/silvermoon>

'No Longer Reasonable': Exploring Feminist Anger

Sarah Cheverton

I am an angry feminist – anger and activism walk hand in hand. Yet as an active feminist in the new millennium, I have often felt the sense of collective anger I associate with the Women's Liberation Movement of the seventies has dissipated over the last three decades. This has raised important questions for me around whether such collective anger has been diluted, or merely changed its form of expression. This piece explores the relationship between feminist anger and the Women's Liberation Movement in an attempt to establish the need for anger in contemporary feminism.

My perceptions of feminist anger in the seventies are directly linked to my understanding of the Women's Liberation Movement, from iconic images of events such as the Miss World demonstrations (1969 and 1970), or the 'Reclaim the Night' marches (Bassnett 1986). My sense of the seventies movement are based on my readings of the seventies movement. As I was born in 1976, nostalgia is not at work here in any simple sense, but I do acknowledge that there is a sort of idealism in my perceptions of the feminist movement of the seventies.

The activism of the seventies, as I read it through the recording of feminist histories, seems to have possessed a collective power that I cannot locate in my experiences. The rhetoric of the seventies movement – its call to all women to challenge the oppression of women through activism – is the source of my belief in feminism. Further, it is an ideal I would be reluctant to lose sight of. Though I still struggle with the 'category' woman, I believe that there is a base to women's oppression, however differentiated in experience, that is related to women's status as women, mediated though it is through race, class and sexuality.

Looking back to the 1970s I feel angry today that in many ways the situation of women has remained the same and the same battles are being fought: violence against women, inequality of status and pay, the sarah cheverton

inequality of caring/domestic responsibilities. I attempt to channel my anger into challenging the causes of women's oppression, by working to improve the situation of women and by attempting to resist the influence of oppression within my own life. My degree in sociology and social policy has been consistently based in feminist theory and practice; I campaign with and for feminist organisations and have involved myself in campaigns which, whilst not affiliated with feminism directly, can be seen as 'feminist work', such as volunteering for a local Domestic Violence Helpline.

It is in these acts of activism that I have experienced collective anger, at the severity of certain cases at the Domestic Violence Helpline or at the sheer pervasiveness of violence against women. However, this was not an experience of feminist collective anger, as the majority of the women volunteers do not identify as feminists, and conceptualise the causes of domestic violence in vastly differing ways. The effects of this as an activist is that it is possible for me to access and to 'do' feminist work in various campaigns, yet harder for me to feel as though I am part of a connected feminist 'movement', as I perceive there to have been in the seventies. This is not to say the movement in the seventies was 'unified' in the UK, there were always struggles over difference, related to class, race and sexuality, but rather that there was more dialogue between these differing strands. It was this dialogue which created the sense of a movement.

106

Although I think feminists are still angry, I propose that, in a sense, getting angry again and being seen to be angry is an answer to the problematic aspects of the fragmentation of the movement. I am suggesting that the source of feminist anger can be reconceptualised, to encapsulate the relationships between different experiences of women's oppression. In wider culture a process of feminist politicisation is failing to happen for a variety of reasons. Feminist rhetoric is employed in so many (non-feminist) contexts that to many women it is meaningless: feminism can be used to justify military action, or to sell shampoo! (See Viner 2002). Feminism has been employed so inappropriately that many women believe it no longer has any relevance, that all gender struggles are now over.

In popular culture the rhetoric of feminism is most often employed to emphasise individualism, not collective action; for example in debates about a woman's 'right' to wear a short skirt, or to define her own sexuality as exemplified in the 'feminism' of *Ally McBeal* or of *Sex in the City*. Yet women are still being raped and beaten, women's work is still shit work, and women are still under-represented within the echelons of male power.

The fundamental bases of women's oppression remain intact, and the representations of *Ally McBeal* feminism serve only to undermine and distract. The 'reactivation' of feminism necessitates the presentation of women's oppression as consistent and dangerous. The majority of women have lost sight of what there is to be angry about.

As I write today, a serial rapist nicknamed the 'Trophy' rapist, who has claimed ten victims so far, fills the news. Police are warning all women and girls across southeast England 'that they should be accompanied and remain alert' (BBC news online), as they have no doubts the rapes will continue. The atmosphere of watchful panic is reminiscent of the fear that spread among women during the attacks perpetrated by the Yorkshire Ripper during the late seventies. Once again, one man sentences the women of the UK to self-enforced curfews and helpless dependency. Once again, one man, portrayed as a monster, reminds women of what we already know: the perpetual awareness of being a potential victim that serves to undermine our autonomy.

I would like to see women stepping out of their houses, together, into the very areas they have been warned attacks may take place. I would like to see large groups of women searching for this man, I would like him to feel hunted and haunted and afraid. Most of all, I would like to see acts of open and furious defiance by women to illustrate that we will not be passively terrified into submission until the burly police force comes to our rescue. In order for this to happen, women would need to link such acts of violence against women with a feminist understanding of women's oppression worldwide. As Solanas fumed in her *SCUM Manifesto* (1968 online), women 'could acquire complete control of this country within a few weeks simply by withdrawing from the labour force, thereby paralysing the entire nation . . . The police force, National Guard, Army, Navy and Marines combined couldn't squelch a rebellion of over half the population, particularly when it's made up of people they are utterly helpless without'.

Bibliography

Bassnett, Susan (1986) *Feminist Experiences: The Women's Movement in Four Cultures* London: Allen & Unwin.

107

sarah cheverton

BBC News Online (2002) 'Girl confirmed as rapist's tenth victim' at <http:/
/news.bbc.co.uk/1/hi/england/2375185.stm> (accessed 30 October 2002).

Solanas, Valerie (1968) *The SCUM Manifesto* at <www.ai.mit.edu/~shivers/
rants/scum.html> (accessed 30 October 2002).

Viner, Katherine (2002) 'George Bush is not the first empire-builder to
wage war in the name of women', *The Guardian* 21 September.

Re-reading the Seventies:
Re-reading Women's Silence

Mary Eagleton

It takes little wit to realise that women's joys are safest when kept secret.

Ellen Galford *Moll Cutpurse: Her True Story* (1993:59)

In this essay I want to re-read the seventies by looking at the motif of secrecy and silence. I want to make two suggestions. Firstly, that the preoccupation with the problem of women's silence and silencing, which might seem at first glance a very seventies concern, has a wider currency and, hence, might lead us to question the tendency to designate periods as expressing discrete kinds of feminism. Secondly, though the dominant seventies line was that silence and secrecy were an imposition on women, they functioned also in other ways and continue to do so. For instance, silence and secrecy can be pleasurable. As Sissela Bok remarks, they can 'delight, give breathing space, and protect' (1986:xv). The idea of the seventies finding silence pleasurable might strike one as odd. It was the period in which women took to the streets, took to the universities, took to a wider job market, all the time claiming that they were here, visible, upfront and demanding to be heard – in short, the end of silence. Very audible demands were made through campaigns around violence against women or the need to recognise the reality of child sexual abuse. Furthermore, this period – and I'm thinking now not only of the seventies – is one in which the therapeutic in various forms has been so prevalent, taking us again in the direction of speech rather than silence. However, I believe there was in the seventies, and remaining with us today, a feminist attraction to silence and I want to explore the problem of that attraction. I am led to these thoughts by my re-reading of a particular text, Ursula Le Guin's short story 'Sur' which was first published in 1982 – so I am already

mary eagleton

taking the liberty of breaking the boundaries of the decade and using a long, or 'longish', concept of the seventies.

The opening words of Ursula Le Guin's short story are predicated on silence and secrecy:

> Although I have no intention of publishing this report, I think it would be nice if a grandchild of mine, or somebody's grandchild, happened to find it some day; so I shall keep it in the leather trunk in the attic, along with Rosita's christening dress and Juanito's silver rattle and my wedding shoes and finneskos. (1985:2008)

The reference to 'finneskos', boots made of tanned reindeer skin, sits oddly with the other contents of the trunk, tokens of a respectable, bourgeois wifehood and motherhood. We read on to find an explanation and discover that we are reading a report by an unnamed, unpublished author who, in August 1909, had set out on an expedition with eight other South American ladies, and reached the South Pole, three years in advance of the Norwegian explorer, Roald Amundsen. Why would the narrator *not* want to publish her report of such an amazing success? A conventional understanding of seventies into eighties feminism would read the story as an illustration of the silencing of women by an oppressive patriarchy. So, one could relate the story to debates on the exclusion of women from representation, or to women's difficult relation to, in Dale Spender's phrase of that period, a 'man made language' (1980), or to the restrictions of male 'gatekeeping', another Spender term. The converse of this view – and, again, common in the seventies and eighties – is the heroic representation of women triumphing over attempts to silence them. The period was certainly preoccupied with women 'finding a voice' (Wilson 1978) and Le Guin's story plays to the interest of the time in uncovering the lives of women 'hidden from history' (Rowbotham 1973). We can recall also the many key texts of the seventies and eighties whose very titles reinforce the view of women as silenced or breaking through silence: not only Dale Spender's *Man Made Language* (1980) but Tillie Olsen's *Silences* (1978), Mineke Schipper's *Unheard Words* (1985), Lauretta Ngcobo's *Let It Be Told* (1987), Adrienne Rich's sequence of poems 'Cartographies of Silence' (1975), Josephine Donovan's essay, 'The Silence is Broken' (1980) or Audre Lorde's essay, 'The Transformation of Silence into Language and Action' (1978).

But looking more closely at the publication history of this listing raises questions and here I come to my first area of concern, how periods are designated. For instance, let's take two of the best-known of these titles. Tillie Olsen's essay 'Silences' started life as an unwritten talk, given at the Radcliffe Institute in 1962 and first published in *Harper's Magazine* in 1965. It was published as part of a monograph with the same title in 1978. Dale Spender's *Man Made Language* was written in 1979, first published in 1980 and both these titles are still being reprinted. So texts that we might initially yoke together as seventies texts with a seventies preoccupation actually have a life that stretches from 1962 to 2002. If we move out of the Anglo-American context and into the French, Cixous' 'The Laugh of the Medusa', her famous exhortation to woman to write, to 'invent for herself a language to get inside of' (1981:257), has a publication history not that dissimilar to Spender's. It was first published in *L'Arc* in 1975 and first published in English in 1976 in the American journal *Signs*. Its Anglo-American market was significantly extended by it being included in 1981 in the first anthology of feminist writing from France, Elaine Marks and Isabelle de Courtivron's *New French Feminisms*. Since then it has been anthologised and excerpted just about everywhere. But rarely have Spender and Cixous been discussed together even though they were produced roughly concurrently and both concerned with women and language. Indeed by the late eighties Spender was being presented as seventies and dated while Cixous was being presented as of the moment. So we conjoin some texts as 'seventies' even though their publication history is much longer and more diverse while with other texts we refuse a commonality as 'seventies' even though their moment of production was the seventies. A history of the production and reception of feminist texts obviously demands more space than can be given here. All one can say at the moment is that it is difficult to see how texts can be demarked by the dates of their writing or first publication, by their periods of influence or by the substantive nature of their content in anything but a tentative manner and part of the problem of the 'decades approach' is its oversimplification of complex and shifting fields of enquiry.

A more productive way of viewing our history might be through Edward Said's concept of 'traveling theory'; as Said says, 'Like people and schools of criticism, ideas and theories travel – from person to person, from situation to situation, from one period to another' (1991:226). Said indicates how these movements may be conscious or unconscious, dependant on attentive reading or indicative of 'wholesale appropriation' (226) and, in the process of the travelling across time and space, the theory or ideas may gain, lose, certainly change, be accepted or resisted, be employed in different contexts with different effects. What I like about this idea is that it seems to guard against the danger of dismissiveness, what E. P. Thompson called 'the enormous condescension of posterity' (1963:12). Rather than seeing feminist history as on an upward trajectory from past theoretical simplicities (the seventies) to present sophistication or from past political inequalities (the seventies) to a current liberation of gender fluidity or, conversely, on a downward trajectory from past political activism (the seventies) to a contemporary apathy and commercialism, travelling theory can encourage us to move both forwards and backwards to see the breaks and continuities in the history of ideas, the political consequences of those ideas and the messiness of an intellectual and political history which, at our peril, we coerce into neatly defined decades. As Bharati Mukherjee has pointed out, the past is too often presented to us with a 'fatal unclutteredness' (1994:6).

So let us do a bit of travelling with Ursula Le Guin to consider again the issue of silence and secrecy. I want to travel back in time as far as 1929 and forward in time to the present. Virginia Woolf offers one possible reason for women's silence in her essay, 'Professions for Women' (1942), and in so doing indicates the constraining aspects of silence and secrecy. She suggests that women writers are 'impeded by the extreme conventionality of the other sex' (1993:105). This is certainly the case for the women in Le Guin's story. The narrator discretely leaves out the surnames of her companions; the women remain silent about the name of their benefactor; they swear to secrecy the captain of the ship which takes them to Antartica; they construct pretexts to cover their absences – retreat in a Bolivian convent or the winter season in Paris – and the reason for all this, the narrator tells us, is lest 'embarrassment or unpleasant notoriety . . . be brought upon unsuspecting husbands, sons etc.' (1985:2010). Evidently, even when women are not talking about sex, which was the focus of Woolf's remark, the delicate sensibilities of men have to be protected; everything from slightly unconventional behaviour to historic achievement is a threat. As Woolf shows in the character of Professor von X in *A Room of One's Own* (1929), that sensitivity can in certain circumstances become violent. Writing *The Mental, Moral and Physical Inferiority of the Female Sex*, he stabs the virgin page with his phallic pen 'as if he was killing some noxious insect as he wrote' (1993:28). Who knows what would happen if the Professor had to write of an incident where women were mentally, morally and physically superior – for example, being the first to discover the South Pole. No wonder the women of 'Sur' decide to leave no mark in the public domain, whether on the land they explored, in historical record or as a personal narrative.

Woolf's comments link readily with those of Joan Rivière and, indeed, Rivière's famous essay, 'Womanliness as a Masquerade', was published in 1929, the same year as *A Room of One's Own*. 'Women who wish for masculinity', Rivière tells us, 'may put on a mask of womanliness to avert anxiety and the retribution feared from men' (1986:35), the retribution of which Professor von X is clearly capable. The conventional behaviour of the women of 'Sur' (the story indicates that the expedition was the only occasion on which they acted independently), the pretexts they devised and the narrator's care to keep the account secret ensure that retribution is kept at bay. The account ends with a note added in 1929 – again the year of Woolf and Rivière:

> We are old women now, with old husbands, and grown children, and grandchildren who might some day like to read about the Expedition. Even if they are rather ashamed at having such a crazy grandmother, they may enjoy sharing in the secret. But they must not let Mr Amundsen know! He would be terribly embarrassed and disappointed. There is no need for him or anyone else outside the family to know. We left no footprints, even. (1985:2022)

The story of the expedition can be revealed only in old age and only within the confines of the family. The threat it embodies to the male reader will there be transformed into harmless eccentricity and years of playing the role of 'merely a castrated woman', 'masquerading as guiltless and innocent' (Rivière 1986:38) will defuse the danger. With age and respectability comes limited licence. Carolyn Heilbrun could have been talking of the grandmothers of 'Sur' when she wrote: 'It is perhaps only in old age, certainly past fifty, that women can stop being female impersonators, can grasp the opportunity to reverse their most cherished principles of "femininity"' (1989:126).

It is not surprising that Woolf, Rivière and Le Guin should fit so neatly together. Though Woolf and Rivière are concerned with women who are moving into what at that time was seen as an almost exclusively male sphere of intellectual pursuits, while the women in Le Guin's story seek to usurp the father's place as adventurer, discoverer, survivor, the texts bring together the periods of first and second wave feminism, the common problems of male power and female vulnerability and the common defensive strategy of silence and secrecy played out as part of the female masquerade.

In another way, though, the women of 'Sur' differ from Rivière's model – and it is here that I begin to move into my second area, about pleasure in silence and the problems of pleasure in silence. The women display none of the distressing psychic symptoms that disturb the women of Rivière's case-studies. This is, I believe, for three reasons. Firstly, though the women are looking to break out of the private sphere, albeit temporarily, they are not concerned about recognition in the public sphere. For Rivière's women it is the public exhibition at the lecture podium or in writing or in giving instructions that render their masculine desires impossible to accommodate. Secondly, Le Guin's narrator shows, in Rivière's words, 'a high degree of adaptation to reality' (1986:36). For her 'the capacity for womanliness' seems more than simply 'a device for avoiding anxiety' (1986:38). Nor does her life consist 'alternately of masculine and feminine activities' (1986:38). Apart from this one momentous occasion the narrator seems to be in happy acquiescence with her lot. The pleasure she can take in her position as wife, mother and grandmother together with her middle-class status may convince her that she has more invested in maintaining the status-quo than challenging it. In this respect, the narrator of 'Sur' is close to Irigaray's description of the masquerade as 'what women do in order to recuperate some element of desire, to participate in man's desire, but at the price of renouncing their own' (1985:133). But, thirdly, rather than merely being victims of the masquerade or unconsciously caught up in its workings, we see the women of 'Sur' using the masquerade as a deliberate and highly effective strategy not only to defend themselves but to reclaim something of their own desires, using it, as Mary Ann Doane believes Rivière failed to, for 'joyful or affirmative play' (1991:38). Judith Butler talks of the 'undecidability' of gender, 'neither a purely psychic truth, conceived as "internal" and "hidden," nor . . . reducible to a surface appearance' (1993:234). This play between psyche/secret and appearance/revealed is 'regulated by heterosexist constraints though not . . . fully reducible to them' (1993:234). In Le Guin's story the undecidability of the masquerade, itself on the cusp of essence and appearance, secret and revealed and also regulated by heterosexism but not reduced to it, can produce both conservative and subversive effects that can be exploited by the women. Hence, the retreat in a convent or a season in Paris is for the men evidence of what women are really like, either virtuous or vain (conservative) while for the women it is a calculated deployment of femininity to enable them to fulfil their own desires (subversive). The masquerade ensures that they retain a feminine and private subjectivity (conservative) but the masquerade might also enable new meanings for femininity (subversive).

The inclusion of the story in 1985 in Sandra Gilbert and Susan Gubar's *The Norton Anthology of Literature by Women* indicates its popularity and how rapidly it reached canonical status within feminism. Le Guin too has made clear her own delight in the writing of 'Sur'. She actually describes it as 'one of the pleasantest experiences of my life'

(1992:172). There is pleasure in the achievement of the women and in the reversal of expectation and hierarchy that the story reveals. As Le Guin comments on her own intentions: 'What I wanted was to join them (*the male explorers*), fictionally. I had been along with them so many times in their books; why couldn't a few of us, my kind of people, housewives, come along with them in my book . . . or even come before them?' (1992:172). That ellipsis marks the moment when the non-heroic housewives surpass the heroic men. In taking the women to the South Pole, Le Guin establishes, in Irigaray's words, '[a] world for women. Something that at the same time has never existed and which is already present, although repressed, latent, potential (1993:109). Like all creative writing, the story allows that imaginative leap into the 'repressed, latent, potential'. The South Pole section of the story shows us the possibilities of a different social order. Unlike the men's expeditions, the women's is distinguished by respectful, creative, at times playful attitudes towards the land and the process of exploration. They have no interest in colonising the land; their mapping consists of making up funny names for the places they discover and the arrival at the South Pole is marked not by the raising of a flag but by the brewing of a cup of tea. Le Guin marries a green politics with the practice of prudent housekeeping; not for these women the disarray of empty meat tins, broken biscuits and dog turds that surround the camp that Scott and Shackleton had used. Their practical good sense copes with everything including a pregnancy and birth. The social relations the women establish of openness and ease, the chain of command that they set up but, significantly, never use, their under-cutting of any pretension question the male heroic ethic of leadership and individualism and, equally, are a long way from the female rivalry Rivière associates with the masquerade.

115

However, the paradox of the story is that it is difficult to see how this new social order could ever find public expression since secrecy is essential – essential to protect it from male retribution but essential also because the secrecy is integral to the women's pleasure. To adapt my epigraph from Galford, it seems that women's joys are not only safest when kept secret but also most pleasurable. It is from the perspective of pleasure that the women's silence begins to look less of an imposition, less of a necessary strategy and, perhaps, less noble. The old-fashioned charm of the narrator hides a more complex structure of feeling and relationship. Her remarks about not wanting to embarrass men, about protecting Mr Amundsen, the decision to leave no mark at the South Pole lest 'some man longing to be first might come some day, and find it, and know then what a fool he had been, and break his heart' (1985:2020), her understanding that 'the backside of heroism is often rather sad' (1985: 2015) reveal her as fully aware, and yet tolerant, of the limitations of male heroism. The narrator expresses both kindness and a knowingness. All the women, it appears, are mothers, indulging the boys' games and safeguarding from attack the tender psyches of their menfolk through a process of ingenious manoeuvring, humouring and, if necessary, 'wretched contrivances and downright lies' (1985:2011). Men might do brave things, the story indicates, but they are emotionally insecure; women are emotionally strong and flexible, adept at coping. Women must maintain their masquerade so men can retain their phallic display. This protective indulgence is similar to Le Guin's own. She describes her goal in writing as being 'to subvert as much as possible without hurting anybody's feelings' (1992:vii) – a goal which is, I believe, just about as achievable as reaching the South Pole hopping on one leg.

What the women of 'Sur' never admit to, nor, I think, would Le Guin is how this knowingness and indulgence is linked to a sense of superiority over the men. Stephen Heath has remarked that among the many possible interpretations of the masquerade is 'subjection to the male régime of "the woman"' but also 'derision of that régime' (1986:47). The women of 'Sur' are subjected, though not without rewards, but they

also see the male régime as risible, so easily fooled. Virginia Woolf asks in *Three Guineas* (1938), 'what possible satisfaction can dominance give to the dominator' (1993:257). We can equally ask what possible satisfaction can dominance give to the dominated. The women of 'Sur' suggest that, when not directly under threat of retribution, dominance can be good for a laugh. In Jeanette Winterson's *Sexing the Cherry*, the same reaction is commented on explicitly by Jordan, a male character, dressed as a woman and moving among women:

> I watched women flirting with men, pleasing men, doing business with men, and then I watched them collapsing into laughter, sharing the joke, while the men, all unknowing, felt themselves master of the situation and went off to brag in the bar-rooms and to preach from pulpits the folly of the weaker sex.

> This conspiracy of women shocked me. I like women; I am shy of them but I regard them highly. I never guessed how much they hate us or how deeply they pity us. They think we are children with too much pocket money. (1989:29)

It is the open display of derision that causes problems. For example, Rivière's patient who cannot prevent herself from interspersing her lecture with jokes and flippant remarks receives in return 'comment and rebuke' (1986:39) from her male colleagues. Secret derision, shared within a chosen circle, has none of the threat and all of the pleasure.

At the end of the story, the women return to their old lives; there is no sense of a wider movement among women. A couple of clues have been left for posterity: the hidden text in the trunk will probably one day be read; the underground ice sculptures that Berta carved will 'last as long as stone' (1985:2016) and so may be discovered. But there is on the part of the narrator no eagerness for this discovery. On the one hand she has a Woolfian indifference to power, honours, publicity, ego; on the other she is adjusted to her social position and in both class and gender terms earns benefits. As Pierre Bourdieu would remark she has made an 'elective renunciation' (1996:28).

For the reader other factors come into play. Is the pleasure of reading this story tied up with a form of *ressentiment*? The slave, Nietzsche tells us, 'has a perfect understanding of how to keep silent, how not to forget, how to wait, how to make himself provisionally small and submissive' (1996:24). The contemporary feminist reader can enjoy how the women of 'Sur' act out their need but much of the pleasure of the story lies also in the not acting out, in the secrecy around the story, in savouring the possibility of a future, explosive revelation of the report and the significant re-writing of history it offers – that is silence, not forgetting, waiting, appearing submissive. This is the 'imaginary revenge' Nietzsche talks of which compensates those 'to whom the real reaction, that of the deed, is denied' (1996:22). Secondly, the difference between envy and *ressentiment* is that the latter rejects the values that it will never be able to attain. The women of 'Sur' don't reject those values but remain largely admiring of the heroic men, holding up the mirror that reflects and magnifies them. It is the contemporary feminist reader who questions that admiration, situates it within a particular class, period, ideology and psychic formation and, thus, is led to reject the men's heroic individualism and expansionism and to value the women's non-heroic collectivism and environmentalism. The *ressentiment* encouraged in such a reading of this story is not of the corrosive, rancorous, poisonous, vindictive, cunning nature that Nietzsche discusses; it is debunking, full of fun, a necessary defence by the powerless. But, then, one may never fully know the forces of repression at play that can lead one to mask pain and rage behind wry humour and gentle mockery. In reading 'Sur', the feminist reader does feel superior to the men who are caught in the absurdity of the bubble of heroic masculinity and their values are diminished; we feel good about the women and we endow them with a superiority they themselves don't want; we also feel good about ourselves, not only in possessing the superior values but in belonging to the 'conspiracy of women' that Winterson mentions. We enjoy being privy to this secret circumvention of male power and, perhaps, remember with some glee our own similar circumventions.

Let me stress what I am and am not saying here. I am not saying that feminism is involved merely in a reactive devaluation of what is unattainable. I am not saying that feminism merely represses its dark desires and transforms them into a form of moral superiority. I am happy to take the moral stand and say that the values of the women of 'Sur' really are better than the men's. Yet it is worrying that the politics of 'Sur' are ultimately so quiescent. How does that come about? We have seen how silence and secrecy are elements in both the masquerade and *ressentiment* and in each case have potential to be both constraining and pleasurable. The masquerade keeps the secret and enables the women's rebellious action. This allows us that inspiring vision of a different world. But the secrecy is also self-defeating. The desire behind the masquerade is never revealed; a change in the social order remains a very distant possibility. As Véronique Machelidon says of Rivière's own project: 'Rivière's artistic creativity and rebelliousness has been subdued into a masquerade that exposes, mocks, but ultimately does not threaten established gender hierarchies and psychoanalytic authorities' (2000:106). The pleasure of secrecy, of collusion and conspiracy can lead us to 'imaginary revenge', away from action, to 'the magnificence of self-abnegating, calm, and patient virtue' (Nietzsche 1996:30), even to a fear of freedom. Ultimately, it is not that pleasure and constraints are in opposition. The secret pleasure becomes disabling and ties us to the constraints. Does the fact that for twenty years now I – and, I'm sure countless others – have found 'Sur' such a satisfying read tell us something about one worrying strand in the trajectory of feminism from the old century to the new?

118

Bibliography

Bok, Sissela (1986) *Secrets: On the Ethics of Concealment and Revelation* Oxford: Oxford University Press.

Bourdieu, Pierre (1996) *The Rules of Art* Cambridge: Polity Press.

Butler, Judith (1993) *Bodies that Matter: On the Discursive Limits of 'Sex'* London: Routledge.

Cixous, Hélène (1976) 'The Laugh of the Medusa' (trans Keith Cohen & Paula Cohen), in Elaine Marks and Isabelle de Courtivron (eds) (1981) *New French Feminisms* Brighton, Sussex: Harvester Press Ltd.

Doane, Mary Ann (1991) *Femmes Fatales: Feminism, Film Theory, Psychoanalysis* London: Routledge.

Donovan, Josephine (1980) 'The Silence is Broken', in Deborah Cameron (ed) (1990) *The Feminist Critique of Language: A Reader* London: Routledge.

Galford, Ellen (1993) *Moll Cutpurse: Her True Story* London: Virago.

Heath, Stephen (1986) 'Joan Rivière and the Masquerade', in Victor Burgin, James Donald & Cora Kaplan (eds) *Formations of Fantasy* London: Methuen.

Heilbrun, Carolyn (1989) *Writing a Woman's Life* London: The Women's Press.

Irigaray, Luce (1985) *This Sex Which Is Not One* (trans Catherine Porter) Ithaca, New York: Cornell University Press.

Irigaray, Luce (1993) *An Ethics of Sexual Difference* (trans Carolyn Burke & Gillian C Gill) London: The Athlone Press.

Le Guin, Ursula (1982) 'Sur', in Sandra Gilbert & Susan Gubar (eds) (1985) *The Norton Anthology of Literature by Women* New York: W W Norton & Co.

Le Guin, Ursula (1992) *Dancing on the Edge of the World* London: Paladin.

Lorde, Audre [1978](1984) 'The Transformation of Silence into Language and Action', in *Sister Outsider* Trumansburg, New York: The Crossing Press.

Machelidon, Véronique (2000) 'Masquerade: A Feminine or Feminist Strategy?', in Peter L. Rudnytsky & Andrew M. Gordon (eds) *Psychoanalyses/Feminisms* Albany, New York: State University of New York Press.

Mukherjee, Bharati (1994) *The Holder of the World* London: Virago.

Ngcobo, Lauretta (1987) *Let It Be Told* London: Pluto Press.

119

Nietzsche, Friedrich (1996) *On the Genealogy of Morals* (trans Douglas Smith) Oxford: Oxford University Press.

Olsen, Tillie [1978](1980) *Silences* London: Virago.

Rich, Adrienne (1978) 'Cartographies of Silence', in *Dreams of a Common Language* New York: W. W. Norton & Co.

Rivière, Joan (1929) 'Womanliness as a Masquerade', in Victor Burgin, James Donald & Cora Kaplan (eds) (1986) *Formations of Fantasy* London: Methuen.

Rowbotham, Sheila (1973) *Hidden From History* London: Pluto Press.

Said, Edward W (1991) *The World, the Text, and the Critic* London: Vintage.

Schipper, Mineke (1985) *Unheard Words* London: Allison & Busby.

Spender, Dale (1980) *Man Made Language* London: Routledge & Kegan Paul.

Thompson, E. P. (1963) *The Making of the English Working Class* Harmondsworth, Middlesex: Penguin.

Wilson, Amrit (1978) *Finding a Voice* London: Virago.

Winterson, Jeanette (1989) *Sexing the Cherry* New York: Atlantic Monthly Press.

Woolf, Virginia (1942) 'Professions for Women', in Rachel Bowlby (ed) (1993) *The Crowded Dance of Modern Life* Harmondsworth, Essex: Penguin.

Woolf, Virginia (1993) *A Room of One's Own* and *Three Guineas* Michèle Barrett (ed) Harmondsworth, Essex: Penguin.

Silence

Hyung-mee Choi

Silence.

Morning. 5 o'clock. I woke up twice last night. What happened yesterday?

He asked me 'why should you go to the conference?'

'Is it important to you?' . . . Silence.

'You have so much things to do. I am also very busy' . . . Silence.

'You even did not finish your dissertation. Others finish it so easily . . . Silence.

'Surely you will find that it is nothing to do with you' . . . Silence

Instead of answering I drank a glass of wine and went to sleep. .

'Do you know I would give up any outing just for this conference this week!'

Bus stop. The timetable told me there was no available bus on the Saturday morning. I should catch the first train.

I could not go back and wake up Him. I was waiting for a bus knowing it would not come . . . Silence.

Over the road, a man started his car engine. I know it is not safe to ask a stranger a ride. But I already ran to the car. 'Puff' 'Sir . . .' I was not late.

Conference. What a wonderful, an intelligent and fancy word it is! Wonderful, powerful women only? Do not be sarcastic. I am also part of this.

I attended with unwanted silence: please speak slowly.

I listened to Mary Eagleton talk about women's silence with silence. 'Feminists recognize silent rage and the pleasure of silence.'

But how can they make political connections with silence? Women are usually forced to be silent. A lot of He have conspired to control women's tongue. Anzaldúa comments that a woman is beaten not because she is lazy but because she talks too much with her neighbour (Anzaldúa 1987).

Behind my silence, there were questions, relief and memories.

Paulina Palmer talked about lesbian mothers. How their economic difficulties worsen their social image. She talked about women who choose sex not for reproduction but for desire. She may be somebody's grandmother. She did not talk about 'once upon time princess'. She talked about our secret desire. Feminist grandmother. Hooray!

Sue Scott and Stevi Jackson discussed 'monogamy'. Within this system, women are oppressed and treated like the property of men. How could feminists deal with 'trust'? These two famous feminists gave us all a chance to laugh. Time passed so quickly. Marriage, love. This was like a chat with my neighbour.

Judy Giles spoke about the 'feminine mystique'. I am sure I am an expert on the 'feminine mystique'. Maybe most women are. But Judy told us about 'Betty Friedan' who was a member of the left wing communist movement. She was not a middle class housewife. She also participated in a political movement for minority ethnic group. She is Jewish and she knew about racism and classism. But she hid her past and pretended to be a middle class housewife and wrote The Feminine Mystique and EARNED a lot of MONEY.

Betty Friedan, a feminist. I believed feminism came from women's real experience. Yet she told of the desire of middle class women. She was able to make feminism popular.

Zoe Fairbairns looked like a girl. She is beautiful and full of curiosity and questions. I recognize her age by her trembling voice.

Gail Chester made us giggle. Her big bubble-like hair, strong eyes and big red trousers. She dared to say she is not an academic person in intellectual conference. I am relieved . . . Me Too.

I came back home at 10 pm.

He was there and asked me why am I so late.

This time I am not angry.

I hide my today's pleasure behind my silent smile.

Bibliography

Anzaldúa, Gloria (1987) *Borderlands/La Frontera: The New Mestiza* San Francisco: Spinsters/Aunt Lute.

This Book Changes Lives:

The 'Consciousness-Raising Novel' and its Legacy

Imelda Whelehan and Maroula Joannou

In Margaret Atwood's *The Handmaid's Tale*
(1985) the heroine is shown old documentary footage in which her mother
and other second-wave feminists ('unwomen') are wearing the kind of
outfit typical of 'unwomen' of their day, dungarees, sneakers and shirts.
Their earnestness, intensity and artlessness provokes the daughter's
amused reaction (Atwood 1985:137). If the word feminism is out of
fashion today it is in part because it connotes the seventies. How can
anything associated with our mothers conceivably be radical, stylish or
chic?

Our concern with the 'seventies' in this paper is with a certain cluster
of fictional works by women which have been variously termed liberation
novels, confessional or consciousness-raising novels and which explore
themes central to debates in the emerging women's movement.[1] They
are especially focused on sexuality and reproduction, love and personal
relationships, women's friendships and the role of the artist in changing
our world-view – mainly the arena of the 'personal' that second-wave
feminists were so keen to politicise in order to theorise and bring about
change. They often used the device of having the central character
'confess', in the form of a retrospective narrative, a diary or memoirs,
her own shortcomings and her own coming to self-realisation. They are
rarely conclusive, but retain a characteristic open-ending.

The confessional novels we discuss are all published in the United
States. The only feminist fiction with a substantial confessional
component that sold in comparable numbers in Britain at this time were
the novels of Fay Weldon, *Down Among the Women* (1971), *Female
Friends* (1975), and *Praxis* (1978). The most famous examples of this

fiction are Erica Jong's *Fear of Flying* (1973), Lisa Alther's *Kinflicks* (1976), Rita Mae Brown's *Rubyfruit Jungle* (1973) and Marilyn French's *The Women's Room* (1977). There are a number of others that have similar concerns and narrative organisation such as Sue Kaufman's *Diary of a Mad Housewife* (1968), Alix Kates Shulman's *Memoirs of an Ex-Prom Queen* (1969), Dorothy Bryant's *Ella Price's Journal* (1972), and Verena Stefan's *Shedding* (1979).

We have been interested in these novels for many years, since we both embarked upon our PhD dissertations in the mid-1980s: two very different doctoral theses, one on feminist consciousness in women's writing during the inter-war period and the other on second-wave feminist thought. We had read and liked each other's work but had never properly met before the Feminist Seventies Conference in York which gave us the idea of working on a collaborative project.

We recognised that the feminist confessions served as surrogate life-stories from the hub of a movement that one of us recognised from personal experience while the other was just a little too young to be directly involved. We were both drawn to analyse the Bridget Jones phenomenon because this is what students in our 'Women's Studies', 'Feminist Thought' and 'Popular Fiction' courses were reading, although neither of us was able to recognise the 'singleton' that peppered its pages in ourselves. What obviously linked the best-selling feminist confessional novels to contemporary 'chick lit' was their massive readerships. We both felt that if we could trace the legacy of the feminist blockbusters to the equally commercially successful works of 'chick lit' we would have a greater understanding of what happened to feminism in the popular consciousness.

There are thematic and structural features which allow us to discuss these novels as a cluster. Firstly, they almost always use the first person for at least part of the narrative. Those that use it exclusively sometimes naturalise its use by presenting the narrative in the form of a diary or memoir. Others play on the intimacy of the first person address to the reader to whom the narrator seems to be directly confessing her secrets. In either case, there is a sense that we are being given revelations which strike at the core of the individual's identity and that gradually these characters will begin to make sense of their lives from a sharper perspective. Sometimes explicitly, but more often implicitly, it is suggested that this will be a feminist one. The novels generally adopt a realist form and concern themselves with 'telling it like it is', offering us views into these women's lives that embrace even the most mundane of details. Like the mothers in Marilyn French's *The Women's Room* their women characters are often depicted as 'drowning in shit and stringbeans'.

The endings of these novels resist closure and are often left open in some way – the protagonists must be shown to be constantly at war with their patriarchal surroundings because to show them emerging victorious would be to stray into utopia – a genre to develop further in feminist writing like Marge Piercy's *Woman on the Edge of Time* (1976). Rather, these women are often on the verge of making a choice, or determining a new beginning; but the clear suggestion is that the reader herself carries this determination forward. At the end of *Kinflicks*, for example, the heroine 'wrapped her mother's clock in her faded Sisterhood is Powerful T-shirt and packed it in Hawk's knapsack with her other scant belongings. She left the cabin, to go where she had no idea' (Alther 1977:569).

The trajectory of the confessional narrative parallels that of the consciousness-raising (CR) group. The author, like a woman taking part in a consciousness-raising group, selects from all the possible events in her protagonist's life those which appear to illustrate her personal philosophy and to have been instrumental in transforming her into the woman whom she has become. Confessional writing proceeded from the subjective analysis of the situations that women experienced in their lives. The central character relates how she has overcome the obstacles which have impeded her own development as a woman and desires to share her new-found understanding with others. These narratives of personal transformation tell of the ways in which individuals became politicised: such writings encourage their readers to believe that more women would find happiness if they too were prepared to break the rules. An endorsement by Fay Weldon on the cover of *The Women's Room* describes it as 'the kind of book that changes lives'.

Books like *The Women's Room* may be associated with what Claudia Dreifus has termed 'soft' rather than 'hard' consciousness-raising: '"Soft" CR was so intensely focused on personal experience that the rules for its practice disallowed theorizing, generalizing and challenging' (Dreifus 1973 in Hogeland 1998:26-7), whereas 'hard' CR required group members to test generalisations on women's personal experience. Thus the raised consciousness of the fictional heroine does not directly lead to collective political action, even though it might result in a shift in consciousness for the individual reader and to a possible association with feminist politics.

The consciousness-raising novels of the 1970s embody a highly personalised notion of the political, of the embattled individual woman witnessing to the 'truth' and swelling the ranks of the growing numbers of women who are determined to stand up and be counted. In some of these novels there is direct contact with feminist characters and ideas but in others the encounter with the women's movement is not explicit. What marks them out as feminist is their use of narrative to make feminist statements about gender and representation. These novels engaged with feminist political questions but tried to work them out through individual experience in terms reminiscent of 'rap' groups[2] in radical feminism for the purposes of consciousness-raising. As Maria Lauret reminds us, Women's Liberation rap groups developed into consciousness-raising groups 'only when generalisations were beginning to be made from women's individual experience to their situation in society at large – a quantum leap from the personal in here to the political out there' (Lauret 1994:63).

Rosalind Coward's oft-quoted essay in *Feminist Review* (1980): '"This Novel Changes Lives": Are Women's Novels Feminist Novels?', a spring board for subsequent discussion on 'what makes a novel "feminist"', was, in fact, a riposte to an article 'Summer Reading' by Rebecca O'Rourke (Coward 1980:53-64; O'Rourke 1979:1-17). Subsequent commentators have felt obliged to revisit Coward's article, but we wanted to take the debate in a different direction by returning to Rebecca O'Rourke. O'Rourke begins with the relationship between her choice of 'leisure' reading and a woman's sense of identity and self: she suggests that summer holidays with their 'promise of time off in near and distant parts' is a time to catch up on feminist publications (O'Rourke 1979:1). O'Rourke recommends as holiday reading Michèle Roberts' *A Piece of the Night*, Marilyn French's *The Women's Room*, Zoë Fairbairn's *Tales I Tell My Mother*, and Alison Fell's *Licking the Bed Clean*, alongside fiction by early twentieth-century women writers issued by the feminist publishing houses Virago and The Women's Press. Winifred Holtby's *South Riding*, and Stella Gibbons' *Cold Comfort Farm* are recommended as part of a project of recovery of feminist writing centred on the women writers of the thirties in order to disprove a hiatus between the 'achievement of full suffrage in 1928 to the beginnings of the current women's movement in the 1960s' (O'Rourke 1979:10-11).

O'Rourke's essay, although lacking Coward's theoretical sophistication, appears to us to contain insights worth retaining, especially in drawing attention to the connections that women perceive between the feminist fiction of the past and the present and those which they make between their preferred reading and the expression of their personal identity. As Anthea Zeman reminds us, the women's novel performed a 'function especially necessary to women; that of telling them accurately where they stood at a given moment', of 'monitoring reports on new freedoms, lost ground, new dangers, new possibilities' (Zeman 1977:2).

The seventies witnessed the emergence of what Lisa Hogeland has termed 'feminist literacy' – the ability to read and understand both texts and everyday life from a feminist point-of-view which does not necessarily lead to political activism (Hogeland 1998:1). The books on a woman's shelves in the seventies were a symbolic marker of her feminist sympathies. Because of the relative scarcity of feminist publications feminists often read everything that came out of The Women's Press, regardless of whether it was fiction or non-fiction. Virtually any book published by Virago in its distinctive avocado-green cover was purchased and read avidly, whether this was a 'modern classic' or a reprint. These included novels like Eileen Arnot Robertson's *Ordinary Families* which appeared to have little or no relationship to feminist ideas.

In *The Re-Making of Love*, Barbara Ehrenreich, Elisabeth Hess and Gloria Jacobs have argued that the sexual revolution of the sixties was essentially a women's sexual revolution and that the changes that this revolution produced in women's lives went far deeper than the removal of sexual taboos and inhibitions: 'if either sex has gone through a change to sexual attitudes and behaviour that deserves to be called revolutionary, it is women, and not men at all' (Ehrenreich et al 1987:1-2). The sexual revolution and much wider access to contraception did not mean that women always experienced sex as pleasurable, or that the new sexual openness eliminated the sexual misery of which women still complained; rather it meant that women felt able to explore sexual feelings and possibilities with greater curiosity, honesty, determination, and candour than before.

In *Female Desire*, Ros Coward argues that the significance of sexual experience for men and women in confessional fiction is different: 'For men sexual encounters represent access to power in having control over women's bodies. Sexual experience in women's novels represents access to knowledge rather than power. Sexual experience becomes the way in which a woman finds out about herself' (Coward 1984:184). The descriptions of heterosexual sex in the confessional novel are as often about sexual failure as success and how women feel that they have been short-changed by normative definitions of penetrative sex. Other sexual episodes are often the means of describing the methods whereby young women are 'educated' into sexual sacrifice. Lisa Alther and Alix Kates Shulman's novels depict the pressure on young girls to 'go all the way' and the time it takes them to find sexual fulfilment or learn about their own bodies. The intention in these scenes and others detailing the minutiae of women's lives is to share experience. The language is often direct and uncluttered, the first person voice less formal, and sometimes humorous, as well as being keyed in to the emotions: it has a certain

129

inclusivity that readers respond to.

Women had inherited a legacy of mistrust and reticence in describing their own bodily parts, fluids and functions. New ways of thinking about the body were demonstrated in Verena Stefan's *Shedding*, which broke the old taboos: 'If I hadn't complicated matters so much carrying my body around a dead weight, if I hadn't lugged it around as I did I would have been more completely co-opted by everyday sexuality. My body kept that from happening. It didn't measure up to male expectations' (Stefan 1979:109). The confessional novels were recognised as displaying a new sexual honesty and explicitness which decoupled romantic love from sex. Women were represented as sexually active rather than passive, depicted as taking sexual initiatives, and using sexually explicit language. The cover of *Kinflicks* quotes a review in *Cosmopolitan* which claims that Alther's novel 'reinforces our new-found knowledge that women can and do write just as powerfully . . . and unsqueamishly about sex as men.' The blurb on the cover of *Fear of Flying* promised the 'sort of absolute candour that for centuries was only permitted to men.'

Fear of Flying details the exploits of a beautiful heroine with an insatiable sexual appetite. The novel's 'deliberate lewdness' (Jong 1998:85) made it perhaps the most controversial of all the consciousness-raising novels. Jong's soi-disant candour has led one of her feminist admirers, Naomi Wolf, to claim that her novels resemble those of D.H. Lawrence 'in terms of originality and honest commitment to voice, rather than in terms of the cheap comparison of their transgressive sexual content' (Wolf in Jong 1998: xv). But other commentators have identified the sexual candour for which *Fear of Flying* in particular has become famed as a 'time honoured confidence trick, with a good eighteenth-century provenance' (Sage 1992:128).

Jong has defended the novel against critics (including many feminists) who saw the book as pornographic, arguing that the 'artist needs to be free to play in the id in order to bring back insights into the ego' (Jong 1998:91), and that 'pornographic art is perceived as dangerous to political movements because, like the unconscious, it is not programmable' (Jong 1998:92-3). Lorna Sage has suggested that what this type of liberation novel gave rise to was Shirley Conran's *Lace*, the 'apotheosis of designer sex (women turn out to want exactly what is on offer, and always better and more)' (Sage 1992:114).

The consciousness-raising novels released women from the prison of decorum and put them in touch with their anger. Anger was *de rigeur* for the feminist writers who came into their own in the seventies although the critical wisdom of the time was that anger was detrimental to the

130

production of good art. The confessional novels acted as consciousness-raisers for an audience who interpreted the experiences of their characters as constricting and oppressive and recognised the causes of their own oppression in the characters' predicaments. These books sold in their hundreds of thousands and the most successful, *The Women's Room* and *Fear of Flying*, in the millions – *Fear of Flying* came tenth on *The New York Times* list of best-sellers in the seventies in the United States (Sutherland 1981:30). It is clear that they generated debates about feminism that extended far beyond the scope of organised feminist politics and into the mainstream media which read their sexual passages as titillating and erotic and who were probably reassured by their heterosexual content. *Rubyfruit Jungle* which focussed on lesbian sexuality was a notable exception to the dominant heterosexual focus of the other confessional novels and acquired its reputation by recommendation within the lesbian community.

Bridget Jones's Diary (1996) has engendered a similar response to the 'that's me' one engendered by the feminist confessional writing. Thousands of readers have clogged the web[3] with their ecstatic responses to the book, and their affirmation that it is an accurate depiction of the single woman in the nineties who desperately wants to find security with the right man and defy the statistics about thirty-somethings. The 'singleton' was born into a world where zipless fucks (a term for quick, impersonal sex used in *Fear of Flying*) are a health hazard in ways undreamt of by Erica Jong and seemingly into a world where feminism had done its work, and in any case 'there is nothing so unattractive to a man as strident feminism' (Fielding 1996:20).

Bridget and her friends are themselves avid trend-watchers and, accompanied by the occasional vaguely feminist rantings of Shazzer, they try to make sense of the world and their own perception of failure in it. The protagonist's failure focuses on two key areas: her body and her love life. Bridget, who lies about reading Susan Faludi's *Backlash* and really reads *Men are from Mars, Women are from Venus* – here the collective consciousness-raising of the seventies is replaced by the individual self-help manual of the nineties – is to some extent aware of the retro-gressiveness of her longings even as her diary records her attempts to improve herself, physically, cerebrally and emotionally. There is little evidence of consciousness-raising along seventies lines: apart from Shazzer's ranting, we have Mrs Jones's Friedan-like discovery of the 'problem that has no name'.

In the diary structure of the novel and the use of humour inviting audience recognition we have a form of writing which seems to hark back directly to the consciousness-raising novels of the seventies. What

131

especially draws the reader into the novel is Bridget's constant failure to live up to the standards to which she aspires. We are reminded that a powerful element of the confessional novels of the seventies was the catalogue of mistakes made by the heroines in their search for self-realisation. To some extent the reader is flattered into thinking herself less disorganised or chaotic than the heroine. Had *Bridget Jones's Diary* been written in the seventies it may well have concluded with Bridget realising how she was duped into trying to conform to unrealisable standards of feminine beauty as well as buying into the myth of romantic love. As it is, the novel enacts a double bluff. The narrative structure sets up a tension between Bridget's sense of her self (fat at just over nine stone) and the fact that the humour partly has to work by us being aware of the extent to which she is deluding herself.

Alix Kates Shulman's *Memoirs of an Ex-Prom Queen*, written in 1969, provides an interesting point of comparison here because the central character, Sasha, also ponders the definitions of feminine beauty and the impossibility of maintaining her former looks:

> Suddenly under the dryer I saw that those very remedies I had come to count on – haircuts, diets, sun, lovers – would produce in time such terrible symptoms of their own that more cures, more tricks, more devices would be necessary to control them. Bleach your hair and it will turn out coarser; shave your legs and it will grow in thicker; have a mole removed and two more will pop out. My own once-radiant skin had begun to show imperfections which to camouflage would be to aggravate. It would dry out in the sun, hang loose if I dieted, puff up if I slept; and even if I did nothing at all, the pores would enlarge, hairs sprout, dimples crease, pimples scar. The whole process was out of control. Once the grey got a start in my hair, it could only spread. And a lover – the ultimate cure was abso-lutely out of the question for the simple reason that I could not bear for him to see my thirty-year-old thighs quiver! (Shulman 1985:265-6)

Whereas Bridget Jones's observations verge upon the celebratory in as much as they confide an experience assumed to be shared by the reader, Sasha offers a lament. The visible signs of ageing intimate why her husband is having an affair with another woman and that the marriage she willingly entered, and the children she willingly bore have entrapped her and reduced her merely to the cipher 'mother'. The women characters in the feminist confessional novels were trying to find new rules of engagement in their relationships. Alix Kates Shulman, a member of the Redstockings feminist collective, famously wrote a 'Marriage Agreement' in 1969 proposing that she and her husband share all household and childcare tasks equally. This document became part of the archive of second-wave feminism. For Bridget as for the characters in *Sex and the City*,[4] relationships have their own rules which they pragmatically accept:

> When it comes to finding a marriage partner, New York has its own particularly cruel mating rituals, as complicated and sophisticated as those in an Edith Wharton novel: Everyone knows the rules – but no one wants to talk about them. The result is that New York has bred a particular type of single woman – smart, attractive, successful, and . . . never married. She is in her later thirties or early forties, and, if empirical knowledge is good for anything, she probably never will get married.
>
> (Bushnell 1997:25)

Bridget's endearing misreadings of her own situation help to explain why Darcy loves her and so the romantic ending (no matter how self-reflexively written) offers narrative closure, despite there being a sequel. Even when Fielding lampoons the Rochester/Heathcliff models of masculinity, the function of the hero remains analogous to his function in Jane Austen or Charlotte Brontë. The novel like much contemporary 'chick lit' displays an awareness of feminism whilst choosing to hark back nostalgically – in Fielding's case to a 'golden age' of romance in the nineteenth-century novel – even though the social codes of Austen's day have long since disappeared.

    If the feminist confessional novels of the 1970s were self-consciously oppositional, the Bridget Jones novels speak to an audience which is decidedly comfortable with the values of Middle England or those of Middle America. Fielding's is the fiction of the mainstream, very distant from outdated notions of collective or radical politics and, above all, from anything that savours of the politics of the ghetto. The contemporary 'chick lit' or 'singleton' writings are marked by their uncritical receptiveness to virtually anything that women may happen to feel or think, irrespective of how self-mutilating, misguided or patently absurd this may be.[5] In contrast to the feminist confessionals of the seventies, these novels not only embrace youth and newness but also, and in ways that would have been difficult to conceive in the seventies, they embrace money, marketing and men.

    This transformational dynamic was physically grounded in the productive and social relationships of women's lives. Whereas the feminist confessionals of the seventies were anchored in the values of the women's liberation movement, the Bridget Jones, 'chick lit' and 'singleton' phenomena reflect the hegemony of the radical right which was established in the eighties and nineties and the *longuers* of successive Conservative governments. The new right were able to establish their ascendency in the cultural and ideological domain in part through their readiness to address issues of morality (such as marital breakdown, the behaviour of adolescents, and the ethics of parenting) that were of general concern. Moreover, their social and economic programmes legitimated acquisitiveness, possessive individualism, and the doctrine that market forces must prevail. The 'sex and shopping' novels, such as Barbara Taylor Bradford's *A Woman of Substance* (1980), provided powerful images of the successful business woman, the 'superwoman' whose power meant taking on the Thatcherite mantle of materialism and ruthlessness. Sexuality did not go away in the eighties although the new woman who enjoyed her power and sex also frequently invested her energies into the quest for money and success. As Jenny Colgan put it in *The Guardian*:

> Growing up in the 1980s all we had to read if we wanted commercial fiction, were thick, shiny, brick novels covered in gold foil, in which women with long blonde hair built up business empires from harsh beginnings using only their extraordinary beauty and occasionally some goldfish. Is it really any wonder we fell on Helen Fielding so desperately? (Colgan 2001)

In the moral climate of Thatcherism the subject of sex was still approached with caution, in part as a reaction to successful public education initiatives warning of the danger of Aids. The Bridget Jones books reflect, among other things, the statistical presence of a sizeable number of unmarried professional women in the eighties and nineties who derive their emotional sustenance from work but whose personal lives are riven with crisis and self-doubt. Bridget Jones, Carrie Bradshaw and the other 'singleton' queens are testimony to the success of feminism: they are independent, in careers, have nurturing female friends. But when it comes to their emotional lives they seem to have problems moving away from a traditional notion of femininity. What is under erasure in the feminist confessional novels, and returns in much of the popular fiction we have discussed, is the desire for romantic love. The dichotomy between these women's success at work and their frustration elsewhere reflects the tenacity of conservative gender precepts. The irony of the

Bridget Jones novels is that younger women exercise power outside the home yet are still bound by men's expectations in the bedroom, and by much the same insecure attitudes to sex as were prevalent thirty years before.

Unlike the heroines of most of the consciousness-raising novels who are escaping marriage and whose sex lives are deeply unsatisfying, these new heroines carry their much vaunted singleness into their thirties. And sex? There is nothing in the contemporary popular fiction which we have discussed to match the inventiveness and exuberance of *Rubyfruit Jungle*, with its unapologetic relishing of lesbian sexual practice and parodic performance of straight sex, or the explicit sexual detail found in *Kinflicks* at the point where Alther mocks the erect penis, the 'size and shape of a small salami, lime green and glowing fluorescently' as her virginal protagonist watches the descent of 'this phosphorescent vision' with the 'absorption of St Theresa, viewing the stigmata' (Alther 1977:126).

Whereas the feminist confessionals of the seventies reflected the need to learn a set of attitudes in order to be part of a movement that spanned generations, the readership of *Bridget Jones* learns a set of attitudes to become part of a thirty-something club. Jettisoned is any notion that the protagonists or authors of a feminist work have to concern themselves with 'feminist virtues' as writers of the eighties and nineties claimed their right to write freed of the encumbrances of affirmation and to explore complexity, ambiguity and the politically incorrect. These tendencies had also been present in some of the earlier confessionals, *Rubyfruit Jungle, Fear of Flying,* and *Memoirs of an Ex-Prom Queen,* which aspired to a particular type of transgression and in their different ways had set out to shock.

Women in the twenty-first century no longer feel the need to justify themselves to the feminist community in terms of their private behaviour or to submit the minutiae of their personal lives to the critical scrutiny of their peers. Vanquished are prescriptiveness in personal behaviour and the 'dictat feminism' that was responsible for translating the popular perception of women's liberation from a positive and promissory term into a joyless fundamentalism that alienated countless women. The extent to which feminists voluntarily abdicated their own individuality in the seventies may be disputed, although one of the authors of this article distinctly recollects a discussion in her own consciousness-raising group in which it was agreed that dying one's hair red with henna was acceptable, while dying it blonde out of a bottle was not! But what many women who are old enough to remember why they became feminists in that decade may now regret is unwittingly providing the ammunition for those who wanted to ridicule any kind of 'education of desire'. As Lucy Burke puts it, the 'spectre of the feminist "folk devil" which haunts the imagination of younger women testifies to the popularly perceived excesses of political correctness and the puritanical curtailing of creativity and freedom' (Burke 1999:9).

The reasons that propelled the seventies heroines into marrying young – non-existent or unreliable contraception, fear of the censure that accompanied promiscuity and illegitimacy and restricted access to the world of work – have on the face of it vanished. Women are doing much better in the public sphere in the new millennium than they did in the 1970s. Women like Bridget Jones have sufficient money and freedom to enjoy themselves as long as they remain childless. However, it remains a fact that the majority of women will have children and that all but a privileged few will have to choose between a career or making their children their first priority, thus facing the prospect of a greatly reduced income for the rest of their lives. This is a choice that seldom presents itself to men in quite the same stark way. Becoming a father makes a negligible difference to what most men can expect to earn in the course of their lives.

Thatcherism accentuated the inequalities and differences between women, the recognition of which had firmly anchored the women's movement of the seventies to political radicalism and the eradication of inequality. This emotive attachment to root-and-branch change was severed in the work of a new group of writers including Rene Denfeld, Katie Roiphe, Natasha Walter and Naomi Wolf who emerged in the eighties and nineties and claimed to represent a glossier and more inclusive variety of feminism and to speak for a new generation of women. The first two specifically set out to discredit the particular brand of feminism born in the late 1960s. Naomi Wolf, as we have seen, claims Erica Jong as her own role model and uses material success or fame as markers for role models for women as does Natasha Walter. Walter was born in the late 1960s and was, like the heroine in *The Handmaid's Tale*, brought up as the daughter of a campaigning second-wave feminist, many of whose attitudes she has rejected. In *On the Move: Feminism for a New Generation*, a collection of essays edited by Walter with contributions by a number of younger feminists, Helen Wilkinson pleaded that we should 'revisit the Thatcher legacy, to approach it with a more balanced mindset, to be honest and generous about her achievements as well as her limitations' (Wilkinson 1999:27-42; 30). Wilkinson saw Thatcher as a 'woman who did not shy away from showing how much she loved power, and in turn she made it legitimate for us to love it too' (Wilkinson 1999:31). Thus Thatcher is rehabilitated and joined by other successful women including Madonna and Geri Halliwell of the Spice Girls. As this model of empowerment suggests, gaining 'control' of one's life comes to mean freedom to dress as women want, drink Chardonnay, define their relationships, and earn a fortune, but without any real concern for the wider world or the women in it. Many of the hallmarks of 'new feminism' represented by Natasha Walter and Naomi Wolf are present in the Bridget Jones books including the fascination of the latter with youth, style and beauty.

The Bridget Jones novels have been used to endorse the sentiments of conservative cultural commentators opposed to the 'over education' of women and advocating a return to traditional gender roles. In *The Miseducation of Women,* James Tooley has invoked Bridget Jones as an example of a modern 'over-educated' woman supposedly dissatisfied with her life and has argued that her education should have encouraged her to pursue the path of marriage and motherhood instead of an emotionally unfulfilling career (Tooley 2002 in Wallace 2002:15). Three decades after black feminism and lesbian feminism have gained some ground in academic feminism, the 'new feminism' returned women to the world of women largely shaped by the needs and experiences of white middle-class women. *Bridget Jones's Diary* can be read as the literary expression of what Adrienne Rich has termed '"life-style liberation", personal solutions to the few – and those few overwhelmingly white' (Rich 1979:309). In the confessional novels of the seventies the home and the inner life of the emotions become the points of departure from which women's lives can be analysed. In the popular fiction which we have discussed these become the means and the end of the narrative: the completion of the self predictably achieved by the acquisition of a steady boyfriend. If, as some media commentators would like to argue, this is a post-feminist statement, let us hope, as Gaby Wood suggested in *The Observer* last year, that 'post-feminism is something you grow out of, in order to become a feminist' (Wood 2001).

imelda whelehan and maroula joannou

Notes

1 For useful discussions of these novels see Gayle Greene *Changing the Story: Feminist Fiction and the Tradition* (Bloomington: Indiana University Press, 1991); Lisa-Marie Hogeland *Feminism and its Fictions: The Consciousness-Raising Novel and the Women's Liberation Movement* (Philadelphia: University of Pennsylvania Press, 1998); Maria Lauret *Liberating Literature: Feminist Fiction in America* (London: Routledge, 1994); Maroula Joannou *Contemporary Women's Writing: From The Golden Notebook to The Color Purple* (Manchester: Manchester University Press, 2000); Lorna Sage *Women in the House of Fiction: Post-War Women Novelists* (London: Macmillan, 1992).

2 'Rap groups' – a term most commonly used in the USA – refers here to the practice within the Women's Liberation Movement (and before that within the New Left) of setting up small localised groups of women who could discuss issues around their own coming to feminism and set up strategies for group action and discussion. They were vigorously female-centred and their main aim was to facilitate consciousness-raising activities in a semi-structured way, so that individual concerns could be seen as having wider social significance. As Jo Freeman remarked, 'The rap groups have become mechanisms for social change in and of themselves. They are structures created specifically for the purpose of altering the participants' perceptions and conceptions of themselves and society at large' (Freeman 1971:3).

138

3 Obvious sources are the online bookseller pages such as Barnes and Noble.com <http://search.barnesandnoble.com/booksearch/isbnInquiry.asp?isbn=014028009X> (accessed 6 September 2002); Amazon.com <www.amazon.com/exec/obidos/ASIN/014028009X/102-8462185-1125757> (accessed 6 September 2002); and Amazon.co.uk <www.amazon.co.uk/exec/obidos/ASIN/0330332775/ref=sr_aps_books_1_2/202-1836539-9635856> (accessed 6 September 2002).

4 *Sex and the City* was first published in the US in 1996 – the same year that *Bridget Jones's Diary* emerged in the UK. Just as Helen Fielding conceived Bridget Jones in her newspaper column for *The Independent*, so Bushnell's novel started life as a column for *The New York Observer*. The novel is effectively a collection of these columns which act as vignettes of the New York dating scene where the same characters regularly crop up – particularly Carrie Bradshaw, Samantha Jones and Mr Big. It is better known through its spin-off TV series which has a cast of more established characters.

5 Other examples of 'chick lit' authors include Jane Green, Jenny Colgan, Lisa Jewell and Melissa Nathan.

Bibliography

Alther, Lisa (1977) *Kinflicks* Harmondsworth: Penguin.

Atwood, Margaret (1985) *The Handmaid's Tale* London: Jonathan Cape.

Burke, Lucy (1999) 'Feminism, Femininity and "The Bridget Syndrome"', *CCUE News*, 11, Summer.

Bushnell, Candace (1997) *Sex and the City* London: Abacus.

Colgan, Jenny (2001) 'We know the difference between foie gras and Hula Hoops, Beryl, but sometimes we just want Hula Hoops', *The Guardian* 24 August.

Coward, Rosalind (1980) '"This Novel Changes Lives": Are Women's Novels Feminist Novels?: a Response to Rebecca O'Rourke's Article "Summer Reading"', *Feminist Review*, 5:53-64.

Coward, Rosalind (1984) *Female Desire: Women's Sexuality Today* London: Paladin.

Ehrenreich, Barbara, Elizabeth Hess, and Gloria Jacobs (1987) *Re-Making Love: The Feminization of Sex* London: Fontana.

Fielding, Helen (1996) *Bridget Jones's Diary* London: Picador.

Freeman, Jo (1971) 'The Women's Liberation Movement: Its Origin, Structures and Ideals', <http://scriptorium.lib.duke.edu/wlm/womlib/> (accessed 9 September 2002).

French, Marilyn [1977](1986) *The Women's Room* London: Abacus.

Greene, Gayle (1991) *Changing the Story: Feminist Fiction and the Tradition* Bloomington: Indiana University Press.

Hogeland, Lisa-Marie (1998) *Feminism and its Fictions: The Consciousness-Raising Novel and the Women's Liberation Movement* Philadelphia: University of Pennsylvania Press.

Joannou, Maroula (2000) *Contemporary Women's Writing: From The Golden Notebook to The Color Purple* Manchester: Manchester University Press.

Jong, Erica [1973] (1974) *Fear of Flying* London: Grafton.

Jong, Erica (1998) *What do Women Want? Power Sex Bread and Roses* London: Bloomsbury.

Lauret, Maria (1994) *Liberating Literature: Feminist Fiction in America* London: Routledge.

O'Rourke, Rebecca (1979) 'Summer Reading', *Feminist Review*, 2:1-17.

Rich, Adrienne (1979) *On Lies, Secrets and Silence: Selected Prose, 1966-1978* New York: Norton.

Sage, Lorna (1992) *Women in the House of Fiction: Post-War Women Novelists* London: Macmillan.

Shulman, Alix Kates [1969](1985) *Memoirs of an Ex-Prom Queen* Chicago: Academy Chicago Publishers.

Stefan, Verena (1979) *Shedding* London: The Women's Press.

Sutherland, John (1981) *Best-Sellers: Popular Fiction of the 1970s* London: Routledge and Kegan Paul.

140

Wallace, Jennifer (2002) 'Sink Schools?', *The Times Higher Education Supplement* 17 May:15.

Whelehan, Imelda (2000) *Overloaded: Popular Culture and the Future of Feminism* London: The Women's Press.

Wilkinson, Helen (1999) 'The Thatcher Legacy: Power Feminism and the Birth of Girl Power', in Natasha Walter (ed) *On the Move: Feminism for a New Generation* London: Virago.

Wood, Gaby (2001) 'Call me a Feminist', *The Observer* 16 September.

Zeman, Anthea (1977) *Presumptious Girls: Women and Their World in the Serious Woman's Novel* London: Weidenfeld and Nicolson.

The Edwardian Lady: A 1970s Icon?

Sarah Edwards

What were the feminist seventies? How can
the feminist seventies be re-read? These key questions prompted me to
lay *The Country Diary of an Edwardian Lady* and its predominantly
female fan communities open to the critical scrutiny of the conference.
It seemed that this was an opportunity to encounter and develop new
theoretical frameworks for understanding a fascinating, but complex
and much-neglected, seventies-based fan movement which has
influenced millions of women for twenty-five years, but whose activities
are alien to many feminists' views of the 1970s.

Edith Holden's phenomenally successful nature notebook, *The
Country Diary of an Edwardian Lady,* was published in 1977. Aided by
an award-winning promotional campaign, it remained at the top of the
Sunday Times bestseller list for longer than any previous book and had
sold one million copies by the end of 1978. The public demand for
information about the little-known author led subsequently to a
biography and television drama; the diary inspired an international tourist
and merchandising industry which encompassed household furnishings,
stationery, cosmetics, and lifestyle books of (to name just a few examples)
knitting, gardening and crafts, which were marketed all over the English-
speaking world[1] (Richard Webb Limited 1987).

The majority of these consumers were women. For Holden's fans,
then, 1977 was the founding moment of a new politics and identity,
which has determined their subsequent lives. Furthermore, many of these
women were highly self-conscious about the diary's success at this
particular time, and developed complex ideas about the significance of
Holden's re-appearance in the 1970s (an Edwardian, middle-class, semi-
professional artist and naturalist). At first glance, their ideas appear to
be derived from conservative discourses, which require unpacking. These

consumers' explicit reflections on the 1970s often employed the vocabulary of aberration and disturbance, while the diary represented, and inspired 'nostalgia' for, a stable essence of Englishness. But although the diary was thus located in opposition to its historical moment of publication, the subsequent industry and types of fan identities clearly drew on contemporary discourses, in particular in relation to conservation, feminism and female inspiration. These women were clearly engaged in generating a set of relations between gender, class and national identity which can enlighten our current re-evaluation of the developments in female subjectivity and political identity in 'the seventies'.

Yet Holden fandom is still flourishing in the twenty-first century, and a theory of nostalgia based purely on the diary's oppositional relationship to the 1970s is no longer tenable. I realised that I must re-visit the original concepts of nostalgia, gender and Englishness and integrate them with the themes of memory invoked within the personal narratives and histories of the fans themselves. To be an 'Edith Holden' fan now involves situating oneself in an historically developing relationship with the industry. How then does the initial moment of the diary's success in 1977 come to be re-assessed? Does it involve a re-evaluation of the late 1970s, and which contexts repeatedly emerge in the fans' narratives?

I undertook interviews and lengthy correspondences with Edith Holden fans in the course of my research, and I soon discovered that certain recurring themes could be extracted from the broader concept of nostalgia: a history of illness; some deployment of Holden's spiritualist activity or vocabulary; a claim for the educative power of the diary; inspiration from Holden for their own artistic endeavours; and a broadly feminist claim for Holden as a 'liberated woman'. To what extent, then, do these women attempt, in their historical retrospectives on their own fandom, to acknowledge the shaping force of the 1970s, and of feminism, in the development of 'Holdenism'?

In this article I outline the initial critical responses to the diary in a variety of journalistic publications; and also offer a reading of the public history of some of the most prominent faces in the Holden industry. I speculate on whether the discourses and vocabulary which these commentators drew on in the 1970s and beyond in a variety of media sources may have influenced the ways in which these women account for their experiences; and I briefly examine some case studies of Holden fans in an attempt to offer some provisional answers to these questions.

Gender, Englishness and the 1970s

In the late 1970s Holden became an icon of rural English gentility with remarkable alacrity. Few people, then or now, recognise Holden's name or know anything about her life. Her iconic status subsumes her beneath her diary, which is a universally recognisable symbol of certain abstract qualities of Englishness: homeliness, insularity, a love for animals, class-consciousness, respectability. This conflation of meanings is summed up in the mantle which was cast upon her from the first reviews from 1977, 'the Edwardian Lady'[2] (Lines 1977). Such a mantle was somewhat ironic, as Holden was a professionally trained artist and schoolteacher from a socialist manufacturing family in Birmingham, who maintained a rigorously intellectual attitude towards the themes deployed in the diary. They were Unitarians who were deeply interested in the scientific origins of nature, and the possibilities of spiritualist practice for reconciling science and religion; and were influenced by the Arts and Crafts movement, and the political possibilities of art for intellectual regeneration.

Initially, I wanted to discover why this context had been erased or mystified in late twentieth-century versions of Holden's life and achievements, and the implications of these transformations for relationships between gender, class, provincial culture and national identity in the 1970s and beyond. I soon discovered that the diary's publication in the Silver Jubilee year of 1977 provoked easy reflections, in journalism and academe, about how the diary chimed with contemporary re-imaginings of the relation between femininity and national identity, which were apparently shaped by 'nostalgia' for an idealised past of Empire and settled class and gender hierarchies, in the imaginary space of a green and pleasant England, before the cataclysm of World War One.

Holden's journal of natural observations, watercolour paintings, country mottoes and excerpts of poetry – a fairly common production for middle-class women such as herself – had been originally entitled, simply, *Nature Notes for 1906*. Thus, the re-naming of the diary, and the marketing strategies employed from the outset of the publishing enterprise, indicate the immediate and widespread recognition that this production was in accord with vague, contemporary ideas about 'Englishness' and 'nostalgia'. For example, only the Italian firm Mondadori were found to be an acceptable choice of printer, as only they could produce a facsimile version complete with 'authentic' yellowed pages, brown edges, etcetera.[3]

In my attempts to theorise the model of essentially English

femininity which Holden and her work seemed to epitomise, I isolated one central recurring paradox. Reviewers hovered between a rapturous appreciation of Holden as a woman with a talent for depicting an idealised or authentic past, and an understanding of her as an amateur lady painter whose diary's success represented the cultural ascendancy of mediocrity in a decade characterised by the decline of stable definitions of nationality.

According to commentators who subscribed to the first opinion, the diary offered an alternative to a grim present. It was thus perceived to exist in a directly antithetical relation to its historical moment of publication. The diary encapsulated a past 'golden age' of essentially rural stability. It was 'an exquisite journal of English country life'. This pleasure was nevertheless tinged with a sadness at its apparent loss, and was therefore a nostalgic pleasure: 'for anyone who mourns the loss of simplicity and understanding of nature, it is a reaffirmation of faith' (Brook 1977). This diary evoked a sensual appreciation: it was a 'ravishingly attractive book' (Brace 1977). As a beautiful object, almost a relic, it was immediately identified as 'an ideal present, the only trouble is that you want to keep it yourself' (Lines 1977). One journalist commented on the recent rise of the book/present conflation and concluded that 'more publicity had made the public more aware of the value of books as presents'. Thus, its potential as a representative object of national qualities was confirmed by the publication of numerous books memorialising the Jubilee year, such as the similarly-named *Country Life Book of the Silver Jubilee* (*Birmingham Evening Mail* 1977).

These critics were concerned with the diary's qualities as a pure representation of Englishness, which were located in its physical properties and the evocative qualities of both text and pictures. Minute analysis of its contents was avoided; the whole was celebrated as an aid to memory. At the same time, these commentators dramatically depicted the 1970s as violent, urban, and disorientated, directly battling with the attitudes to gender and class which the diary and popular depictions of the Silver Jubilee instilled. In this version, then, the diary is imbued with Holden's active presence, 'vying for supremacy with rampant sexuality, crime and the violence of this age she never knew' (Brook 1977). In its successful vanquishing of this degeneracy, albeit for a few moments of contemplation, it is frequently described as having a medicinal effect: 'it's a nice, safe book, which people may see as an antidote to the sex and violence around' (*Sunday Independent* 1978).

Paradoxically the very 'ordinary' qualities of this private notebook render it unique in this context, and thus inspire extraordinary feelings in the reader. Representations of other women in the media seemed to confirm that a particular combination of feminine qualities is an essential element in many discourses about Englishness, which repeatedly cluster around the concept of the 'ordinary'. For example, Holden has been described as 'a very simple woman . . . in the best sense of the word' (Roberts 1977). Similarly, in 1977, the Queen was characterised as 'simple, exceptionally steady, rock firm, decent'[4] (*Sunday Times* 1977). The middle-class English femininity of these women (and Holden's perceived extension, her diary) reconcile the apparent paradox of the extra/ordinary. They embody an extraordinary or exemplary degree of ordinariness which sustains the stability and order of national identity: they are decorative, non-intellectual, maternal in their responses to the lower creation. They represent an historical order in the midst of the political flux of the 1970s, obliquely referred to, and simultaneously demonised, as 'sex and violence'[5] (Brook 1977; Taussig 1977).

An implicitly feminine 'nature' is thus constantly invoked as an idealised alternative to disturbances of literal and imaginary boundaries. A typical reflection on the memories the diary inspired is the following, in which Englishness, nature, order, didacticism and nostalgia are combined. The reviewer longs for 'the secure England of 1906', when 'British confidence saw "God in his heaven and all right with the world"'. Gender is included in these concepts of the 'natural' hierarchies (Roberts 1977). For example, my next quotation progresses from an implicitly feminised view of nature, to its mimetic recording by a woman who mirrors her surroundings and confirms its gendered qualities: 'there is beauty in simplicity and simplicity in beauty. The natural world about us confirms this' and 'so does a book that chronicles this same world through the brush and pen of a young woman' ('J. T. C.' 1977). These, then, are the network of general assumptions about the components of an ideal Englishness, and recent transgressions from this ideal.

However, broadsheet critics approached the diary as a text and undertook close readings informed by canonical literary values. For these commentators, the work's generic heterogeneity, lack of originality (especially its use of texts by other authors, such as Romantic and Victorian poets including Wordsworth and Tennyson), its alleged botanical inaccuracies and Holden's enigmatic impersonal tone were features which condemned the work as too 'ordinary' – 'it is not a great literary or historical discovery' (Brace 1977). In this context, it became evident that the cluster of concepts and values attached to the 'ordinary'– such as predictability, repetition, comforting stability – invoked extreme ambivalence about the worth of non-canonical female artistic production. One reviewer claimed women such as Holden were 'faintly sad in their concentration on the trivia of daily life' (Hall 1977).

Such speculation about the author often incorporated a proto-feminist consciousness of Holden's gender as an important factor in the production of such a diary. The 1970s were, of course, a key moment in feminist and women's publishing with the founding of Virago and The Women's Press in the early part of the decade. Many forgotten, non-canonical Victorian women writers were published, including other middle-class women who worked as 'amateur' painters and naturalists, such as Marianne North and Margaret Fountaine.[6] Many assessments of Holden were by women, some of whom worked as academics; their assessment of the diary seemed to indicate their interest in 'ordinary' women's writing. For example, Marian Elizabeth Strobel was 'a member of the Department of History at the Phillips Exeter Academy, Exeter, New Hampshire' who noted 'the only option open to women' was 'to concentrate their efforts on such genteel hobbies. Edith's experiences did not waver from this pattern' (Strobel 1980).

One senses an awareness of early second-wave feminist influences in reviews such as these: the work in the diary is partially excused its faults due to the historical moment in which it was produced. But while this kind of commentary entailed a self-conscious acknowledgement of women's disadvantages, it did not extend to a revision of categories. Instead the image of the 'extraordinary woman' was invoked to deny the role of constricting material circumstances for the truly gifted. One male reviewer confidently and explicitly used the binary to justify his critical judgement on Holden: 'lest anyone should think this exceptional in an Edwardian woman' the Victorian painter and naturalist Anne Pratt, author of the more self-consciously 'academic' four-volume *Flowering Plants,* produced 'adventurous, sceptical, inquisitive' natural history, so why not Holden (Mabey 1977)? These reviewers do not consider the material conditions in which the work was produced and the writer's ends, and then consider appropriate methodologies to assess its meaning and significance. Rather they invoke, and appear to celebrate, the category of the ordinary only to re-situate it firmly on the negative side of the aesthetic equation.

In the subsequent decades of the twentieth century, it has increasingly been observed that much early second-wave feminist work is influenced by canonical literary values, due to the white middle-class origin and education of the earliest critics, who, ironically, often reinstate traditional frameworks on different subjects. Notable women of achievement have been 'recovered' as feminist icons and held up as proof of women's intellectual potential. For example, Elaine Showalter's *A Literature of Their Own*, which was also first published in 1977, contains early feminist re-evaluations of 'great women' such as George Eliot. While this is an understandable beginning in the 'gynocentric' project, it is not helpful for an assessment of Holden. Her re-arrival in the late 1970s coincided with only the beginning of scholarly interest in the productions of 'average' women. So feminist reactions to her reflect the features of this transitional period: an uncertainty as to the 'status' of an artist like Holden within a feminist project and the lack of an adequately developed and appropriate critical apparatus to begin to assess her. Thus in 1977, her work produced a similar reaction of confusion for feminists as it did for male critics.

This, then, is a brief summary of the general network of journalistic responses in the late 1970s, which I hope demonstrates how the diary strongly chimed with, and produced new reflections on, discourses about the state of the nation, the significance of the Jubilee rhetoric, and the varying impact of second-wave feminism in different journalistic contexts. To what extent, I now ask, do 'Holdenists' problematise the initial reviewers' assessment of Holden's appeal and, more generally, the academic literature on women's patterns of consumption, fandom and identification (Jenson 1992; Fiske 1992)? The incredible longevity of Holden as icon cannot be over-emphasised. Although the merchandising industry has a smaller turnover today than it did in the 1980s, Holden's fan base is engaging in new areas of activity, such as the creation of personal web pages and the collection of merchandise. Are these re-evaluations of the origins of their enthusiasm in the 1970s entirely suffused with a rosy apolitical nostalgia for the diary's re-appearance? Or is this a simplistic and patronising assessment of nostalgic narratives, which may provide valuable and nuanced accounts of subjective experience?

The success of the diary, and the immediate establishment of the merchandising industry, meant that retrospectives on these events were being published within a year, and incorporated into the publication material. Thus, from the beginning, nostalgia for the Edwardian period was conflated with nostalgia for the diary's discovery and success in the 1970s. One of the simplest examples of this trend is that even the shortest, and most obscure, newspaper articles on Holden commonly provided a teleological history of the diary's discovery and publication. These were explicitly recognised as narratives, as another rendition of the 'Country Diary story'.[7]

Thus the diary soon becomes implicitly identified with, rather than presented in opposition to, the historical moment of 1977: 'it was unquestionably the book of the decade'[8] (Portsmouth: Holbrook and Son Limited 1987). This identification is frequently achieved through the medium of Rowena Stott, Holden's great niece by marriage. One of the core features of this narrative is a teleological thrust, which is here employed to enable a re-telling of the lineage of the Holden family, and which locates Edith as the founding subject, or origin, with Rowena as heir. The discovery of Edith's diary by Rowena is made to seem inevitable: 'for seventy years it had been kept as a family curiosity – nothing more' but then 'the country diary tumbled out of a trunk and . . . Rowena claimed it' (Haddon 1977; Shepherd 1989). Furthermore, the historical moment of this discovery is noted with curious, even pedantic, precision: 'on March 29th 1976 Edith's great niece Rowena Stott arrived at Richard Webb's Exeter home clutching her great aunt's leather bound diary in a brown paper bag' (*Exeter Express and Echo* 1984). A direct relationship is thus developed between these two women, who never met: 'when the Warwickshire artist Edith Holden compiled an anthology of nature notes, she could not have guessed that seventy years later, thanks to her great niece Rowena Stott, it would become a worldwide bestseller' (Shepherd 1989).

In these narratives, we can observe that this identification is attempted by superimposing 'olde-worlde' images of family trunks and brown paper onto the contemporary figure of Rowena. These narratives locate Rowena as Edith's modern incarnation using similar strategies to the reviewers who position Holden and her diary as the epitome of Englishness. Paradoxes and antitheses achieve synthesis through the mediation of middle-class English femininity which transcends contemporary context by virtue of its ahistorical stability. Thus, it is repeatedly stressed that Rowena herself is a shy, isolated painter of delicate watercolours; she has been told she resembles Edith in spite of the fact that they are only related through marriage. The spiritualist context is then invoked to aid this identification: a medium wrote to Rowena to inform her that she was Edith's reincarnation, no doubt spurred on by marketing claims that Edith has 'come back' through her diary.[9] In this discourse, then, Holden is located as a transcendent essence of national identity who can permeate not only contemporary objects such as her diary, but also living persons. Remarks made by Rowena in press interviews are invoked out of context to re-enforce her spiritual link with Edith and her diary – 'it followed us around' and 'I took it over when I was little, because I liked it and used to copy from it' (Shepherd 1989). It seems that Rowena, then, is located as a contemporary role model of feminine and artistic integrity, a champion for the diary's educative powers in the unsettled 1970s.

This teleological emphasis gains in prominence throughout subsequent years, as stress is increasingly laid on the ways in which the diary's success has influenced Rowena's personal development. It is constantly reiterated in 1980s retrospectives that she 'is unspoiled by success'. Narratives are still produced which place the diary in antithesis to current values: for example, in 1982, we have the claim that 'no one has the discipline today to keep such a complete, detailed and illustrated diary as Edith Holden did'. But the same article also details, with minute precision and with the most enthusiastic admiration, the thirty million pounds worth of sales in America of *Country Diary* products. The impact of the diary on Rowena's personal development has been, bizarrely, to transform her into a money-making entrepreneur, one of the first successful purveyors of the 1980s trends of lifestyle marketing, of which the diary both partook, and helped to influence. According to one journalist, Rowena

> initially . . . found it quite alarming dealing with the wheeler dealers in the marketing world. But Richard Webb has guarded and guided her interests over the last five years and Rowena now feels more confident to express her own opinion and veto any products she doesn't find up to scratch. (Galbraith 1982)

In other words, as a 'moral' capitalist, Rowena safeguards her aunt's artistic integrity and her family inheritance, and uses the tools of marketing in order to educate the public: 'she retains a touching belief in the qualities of her great aunt's work' (Galbraith 1982).

149

We have here a new alignment of morality and capitalism, founded by a woman of substance in the dark days of 1977 – which are then paradoxically cherished as the beginning of reformation! This formation of nostalgia, whereby apparently antithetical contemporary discourses are constantly absorbed into re-imaginings of the past, clearly problematises traditional accounts which criticise the emotion as regressive, static, ahistorical in outlook and inhibiting of creativity (Adorno and Horkheimer 1944 in During 1993). We need to consider, then, to what extent Holden enthusiasts themselves assess the influence of the 1970s on the industry and on their own enthusiasms; and how an understanding of this influence might enable a re-evaluation of Holden 'fandom', an activity which has inspired strikingly similar criticisms.[10]

My personal contact with self-identified Holden enthusiasts largely came about through a television appeal on a Channel 4 television programme about fandom, *Collectors' Lot*; I also placed newspaper advertisements and made further acquaintances with the help of the Holden family. I was thus able to interview, or enter into correspondence with, nearly thirty men and women. When I analysed the types of fan responses I was able to broadly divide the people I met into local history enthusiasts, collectors of the merchandise and a small group of women who partook to some degree in all areas of these enthusiasms, but also had a well-developed emotional engagement with Holden. I will now briefly attempt to unravel the complexity of two of these women's responses.[11]

Victoria Williams is a fan who tells her story in a 1985 newspaper article, entitled, 'diary of happy couple who escaped the rat race'. As the title indicates, this is another teleological account centred on a life-changing, epiphanic moment which occurred in the year of the diary's publication, 1977: 'it was a chance meeting in a Brighton restaurant that was to change her life'. The theme of physical suffering, and consequent emotional and artistic deprivation, is strongly foregrounded in this account. She recounts that she was unable to become a concert pianist due to attacks of arthritis. Nevertheless, she possessed an 'obsessional love for the country' coupled with artistic talent. She had never been able to obtain formal art training, but this did not prevent her from drawing wildlife. She later visited a Scottish island, which she found to be a source of great artistic inspiration – she was 'enchanted' with its 'peace, solitude, beautiful scenery'. This feeling was overlaid with implicitly spiritual/spiritualist overtones, which were deeply positive and encouraging: she was 'haunted by the feeling that one day she would return'.

In 1977, she met and married a man who 'loved nature, music and art'. This was the year that Holden's diary was published and 'it was when Victoria saw that book she felt she must create something similar'. She became ill again; they spent their honeymoon on the island and later moved there permanently. So we have the same paradox: the nature diary apparently exists in antithesis to the 'daily rat race of urban life', yet Williams' enchanted life began in the year of its successful marketing, 1977. She attempts to abolish this paradox by creating another: while emphasising this date as the focal point of her life (story), she simultaneously denies the historicity of her account. Instead, Williams invokes the concept of destiny, and more specifically, the features of a ancient, teleological and often ahistorical narrative form, when she claims her life 'took on the qualities of a romantic novel'. She attempts to obliterate her own agency, when instead she could have chosen a narrative form which emphasised her initiative and courage in deciding to move to a remote island. Yet in spite of this emphasis, her invocation of the diary's marketing strategies demonstrates that their own developing discourses of female passivity do celebrate the educative powers of the work of an ordinary woman such as herself – her own diary 'was not meant for publication, but publishers thought it deserved a wider audience'. In another paradox, this type of passively inspired, ahistorical artistic production, when disseminated, is confidently hoped to produce far-reaching didactic effects within a particular historical moment (Leigh 1985).

Carol Andrews, by contrast, is one of the most active and well-known Holden fans. She bought the house where Holden wrote the diary, and has restored its Edwardian character. She has written, and been the subject of, many local journalistic accounts of her fan activities, and the meanings she attaches to them. Yet again, her fan identity is centred around an epiphanic moment in the 1970s and is constructed as a teleological narrative of progress towards an ultimately stable identity. As such, her own relationship with the house is described using the vocabulary of a marriage, which will ultimately provide emotional completion. In the beginning she feels an emotional void – 'we had searched for four long years for an old house with character in Solihull' (Andrews 1980). However, when she sees the house, she instinctively recognises her destiny: 'it was love at first sight – in June 1979' (Freeman 1983). Finally, her story has a happy ending: 'it is November. Sixteen happy months have elapsed since first I saw and fell in love with Gowan Bank' (Andrews 1980). The idea that Carol and Holden's house are destined for each other is re-enforced by her oft-repeated claim that the current owners had feared its fame might attract the wrong buyer, but 'when they saw how much we liked it, the people who lived here before told us Edith Holden had lived in the house. They wanted us to have it' (Harris 1989).

151

Andrews, like Rowena, arrives as a saviour, in this instance to lovingly restore Holden's house. Like the diary, this house is constructed as another site of Holden's ongoing influence, by means of the spiritualist context. Furthermore, by living in Holden's house, Andrews can also create a spiritual, familial lineage between herself and Holden. She has been 'inspired' by the room in which seances were held – she is 'conscious of a strange sensation in the room ever since they moved in' (Freeman 1983). This word, 'inspiration', has both artistic and spiritual overtones within Holden culture, which cannot easily be disentangled. But this seems almost inevitable within the discourses of 'Holdenism' – predictably, the result of Andrews' inspiration has also been a burst of creative activity – 'to write, paint, restore, garden, research and teach' (Walker 1989). However, despite this intense activity, she similarly downplays her own agency by disclaiming sole responsibility for these productions. Yet, as the spiritual vessel for Holden's message, she assumes the right to influence others and her activity within this sphere is unproblematic.[12] Her educative aims are also strongly emphasised, and

are located in the preservation of the local community: 'only recently
have people realised the beauty of Victorian and Edwardian
houses . . . developers have demolished beautiful buildings in recent years,
for example Edith's school' (Freeman 1983).

What can we deduce from these accounts? In some cases, the
influences are obvious and would be openly acknowledged by the fan
communities. We can easily observe the growth of the conservation
movement as a factor in the diary's success, for example. But this was
perceived as a welcome revival of a past national pride in the rural.[13]
What, though, of more controversial feminine identities and the impact
of apparently 'new' discourses of contemporary feminism – how do the
Edwardian and the modern woman compare? These women acknowledge
Holden as an artistic foremother, and thus participate in the re-evaluation
of ordinary women's writing. Certainly, they acknowledge the worth of
these productions in their own celebration of Holden, her inspiration
for their amateur projects, and their often enthusiastic participation in
the merchandising industry, which promotes ordinary domestic crafts.
The disabilities suffered by many fans who feel they cannot become
'exceptional' women shows the importance of role models like Holden.
Holden's fans make creative use of a diary which feminist critics have
been unable to appreciate. Although the diary seems to represent
regressive nostalgic trends, its use by its female fans questions hierarchical
and canonical models. The entrepreneurial activity of these fans, however
questionable politically, asserts the worth of a feminine presence in the
public sphere. For these women Holden is the ideal of a 'liberated woman'.
Hence, the vocabulary of their accounts, which encompasses restoration
and sales figures, all indicate the influence of feminism, emerging
enterprise culture, and women's writing, which inevitably modify and
politicise the supposedly apolitical Edwardian rural idyll they are drawing
on.

Yet at the same time, there remains a profound ambivalence about
any self-conscious acknowledgement of a 'feminist' identity. These
women invoke the concepts of the 'timeless' and 'universal' because
they are committed to the idea of an apolitical culture, which incorporates
many of the discourses about 'essential' femininity that the reviewers
draw on. Their view of history is inflected with the concept of 'destiny'
which downplays the role of human agency in historical process. For
example, the spiritualist context is invoked to suggest that the past is
not 'history', that the spirit of Holden and the values she represents are
eternally present. The majority of Holden fans condemn any form of
relativism, perceiving this stance as fickle and morally bankrupt rather
than an acknowledgement of the mutability of any culture or ideas. For

them, English femininity is a complex and adaptable – rather than mutable – character which weathered the storm of the seventies and made its mark. The renaissance of Edith Holden in the 1970s is thus perceived as a dynamic revival of the feminine principle. This is their collective re-reading of the feminist seventies.

Notes

1 In 1976 Holden's great niece, an art student, had approached the publishers Richard Webb and Delian Bower who, after testing the market in New York and exciting keen competition from many London firms, published the diary with Michael Joseph. It was also published in the USA by Henry Holt and Co.

2 The first reference I discovered was written just one month after publication.

3 The *Sunday Times* magazine bought the serial rights and offered to print an article over the Easter holiday weekend of 1977. The print run of the diary took place in Italy, so to arouse the interest of reviewers a calendar using the diary's illustrations was produced. After this, major bookshops including the National Trust and W. H. Smith started ordering thousands of copies of the diary. Extracts from the book were sold to *Homes and Gardens, Illustrated London News* and the *Birmingham Evening Mail.* Finally posters and carrier bags were produced decorated with the diary's illustrations. The book entered at number one on the *Sunday Times* bestseller list, where it remained for a record-breaking sixty-four weeks. It won the Publisher Publicity Circle award for best book promotion of 1977.

4 1977 was the year when a British woman, Virginia Wade, won the Wimbledon tennis championships, themselves a location of English pride. The connection with idealised national identity and femininity was repeatedly made; for example, 'nobody knew or cared whether the hymn (*Land of Hope and Glory*) was for the Queen of England or for the new Queen of Tennis' (*Daily Telegraph* 1977: 2 July).

5 For example, Ellen Taussig complains about 'days of voluminous print devoted to violence, sex and suspense'.

6 Marianne North's travel writings and botanical paintings were published as *A Vision of Eden* in 1980, and North and Holden were the joint subjects of a review article (Engen 1982). Margaret Fountaine (author of the diary *Love Among the Butterflies*) was favourably compared to Holden, as 'a wonderfully wayward lady who decided early in life', 'to go her own way' in contrast to that 'total nonentity' Edith Holden (Parker 1980).

7 For example, 'A book for all seasons – the *Country Diary* story' (Swedlin 1977).

8 Richard Webb, one of the diary's publishers Webb and Bower, on the 'magic ingredient of *Country Diary's* popularity'.

9 For example, there is an account of the 'reincarnation' (Shepherd 1989). For an example of the discourses surrounding Edith's 'return' through her diary, see Nicholas Jenkins: 'Edith Holden was a spiritualist who always said she would return to visit this world after her death. Edith died in 1922 but now she has come back' (Jenkins 1977). Haddon also speculates that 'in a way her promise has been kept, not by seances and automatic writing but by the diary she kept seventy-one years ago' (Haddon 1989).

10 See the account of 'heritage' in general, and Holden in particular, in Hewison, 1987.

11 Some names have been changed to protect the privacy of individuals.

12 For an account of how nineteenth century mediums such as Holden achieved 'power through passivity' see Owen 1989.

13 For example, the following comment is representative: 'today, Edith would surely have been among the conservationists' (P. L. 1977).

Bibliography

Anon (1977) *Daily Telegraph* 2 July:no pn.

Anon (1977) 'Strange success story of the past year', *Birmingham Evening Mail* 22 December:no pn.

Anon (1978) 'Edith's Edwardian Diary Becomes A World Classic', *Sunday Independent* 12 November:no pn.

Anon (1984) 'The Country Diary of an Edwardian Lady', *Exeter Express and Echo* 23 February:no p.n.

Anon (1987) The Country Diary Collection, '*A Creative Promotion' Advertisement Feature* Portsmouth: Holbrook and Son Limited.

Anon (1987) *The Country Diary Collection Tenth Anniversary Promotion Package* Richard Webb Limited.

Adorno, Theodor and Max Horkheimer (1944) 'The Culture Industry: Enlightenment as Mass Deception', in Simon During (ed) (1993) *The Cultural Studies Reader* London: Routledge.

Andrews, Carol (1980) 'A Home with a History', *Warks/Worcs Life* 27, 9:64-5.

Brace, Keith (1977) 'Fragrance From the Fields of Edwardian Olton', *Birmingham Post* 18 June:2.

Brook, Danae (1977) 'A Country Romance Blossoms Again After Seventy Lost Years', *Daily Express*, 1 July:no pn.

Engen, Rodney (1982) 'Some Diaries of Victorians and Edwardians', *Book World Advertiser* May:6-7.

Fiske, John (1992) 'The Cultural Economy of Fandom', in Lisa A Lewis (ed) *The Adoring Audience: Fan Culture and Popular Media* London: Routledge.

Freeman, Penny (1983) 'In Love', *Solihull Times* 4 March:20-1.

Galbraith, Angela (1982) 'Now you can get into bed with the Edwardian Lady', *London Evening Standard* exact date unknown:no pn.

Grigg, John (1977) *Sunday Times* 29 May:no pn.

Haddon, Celia (1977) 'A Country Bouquet', *Sunday Times Magazine* 17 April:80-92.

Harris, Gillian (1989) 'House Where Time Stood Still', *Birmingham Evening Mail* 12 November:18-19.

Hewison, Robert (1987) *The Heritage Industry: Britain in a Climate of Decline* London: Methuen.

Hodge Hall, Barbara (1977) 'Country Diary is Delightful', *Buffalo Evening News* 11 September:no pn.

Jenkins, Nicholas (1977) 'How Edith returned through the diary that's a smash hit', *Sunday Independent* 25 September:22.

Jenson, Joli (1992) 'Fandom as Pathology: The Consequences of Characterisation', in Lisa A. Lewis (ed) *The Adoring Audience: Fan Culture and Popular Media* London: Routledge.

'J. T. C.' (1977) 'A Gentle Recorder of Nature's Special Magic', *Western Morning News* 1 July:no pn.

Leigh, Vanora (1985) 'Diary of Happy Couple Who Escaped the Rat Race', *Brighton Evening Argus* 23 July:no pn.

Lines, Charles (1977) 'Another World Without Fumes and Motorways', *Solihull News* 2 July:12.

Mabey, Richard (1977) 'A Fastidious Pen', *The Times* 16 June:14.

Owen, Alex (1989) *The Darkened Room: Women, Power and Spiritualism in Late Victorian England* London: Virago.

Parker, Derek (1980) *The Times* 21 November:no pn.

'P. L.' (1977) 'Memories of a Gentler Way of Life', *Sheffield Star* 4 July:no pn.

Roberts, C. V. (1977) 'Evoking One Idyllic Year', *Eastern Daily Press* 13 June:no pn.

Shepherd, Rose (1989) 'Fieldfare and Meadowsweet', *Sunday Times Magazine* 17 September:76-80.

Strobel, Marion Elizabeth (1980) 'The Edwardian Lady: the Story of Edith Holden', *Bestsellers' Monthly* December:no pn.

Swedlin, Rosalie (1977) 'A Book for All Seasons – The *Country Diary* Story', *The Bookseller* 3 September:no pn.

Taussig, Ellen (1977) 'Edwardian Lady Speaks to Us', *Buffalo Evening News* 5 November:no pn.

Walker, Hannah (1989) 'Edwardian Style for this Lady!', *Solihull News* 15 October:21.

Travelling with Joni

Sue Thomas

Joni Mitchell has been a constant presence in my life for many years. I can't even remember when I first discovered her songs but somewhere along the way I acquired several of her albums, the best of which are *Song To A Seagull* (1968) and *Blue* (1971). They have travelled with me for a long time.

In the late 1970s I lived in the suburbs of Nottingham with my then husband and our two small daughters. I was an earth-mother and rather enjoying it. But at some time during those years my husband made a comment which has stayed with me ever since. I was doing the family ironing and, as usual, playing a Joni Mitchell record to sing along to while I worked. It was probably the first album. Yellow, psychedelic, flowery, Side 1 was prefaced 'I came to the city' and Side 2 'Out of the city and down to the seaside'. Songs of streets and beaches, leavings and lovings. Which one I visited depended on my mood, it switched from one to another. That day, as I sang to the speed of my iron, my husband walked into the room and commented bitterly 'I know why you play Joni Mitchell songs - it's because they make you feel free.'

I was surprised. I'd never thought of it like that. This music signified no conscious desire to do anything beyond experience the joy of listening to it. I didn't feel especially trapped at the time, but in fact he was correct to be suspicious. Even then, our marriage was imperceptibly disintegrating and in 1984 it collapsed completely.

After the break-up I took great pleasure in using those long evenings alone after the kids had gone to bed to rediscover who I used to be. I played my records and spent a lot of time on the shoreline with Joni, but never had any curiosity about which beach she was singing about or where it might be. It was, indeed, just the place where she - and I - could be free. An abstraction of light and sand and ocean, lovers, and friends.

Move on a few years more, and I had become a writer. Joni had no presence in my first novel but when I came to write my second, *Water*, a story of love and sex and the sea, I suddenly found myself listening to *Blue* all the time. In the book I wanted to quote her line about songs being like tattoos but when I checked the rights I found I couldn't afford even that one single line of lyric. So I forswore it. But is it a coincidence that on the day of publication, hours before my public reading and launch party, I was suddenly impelled to rush out and have a large and complex tattoo inscribed onto my forearm? Was Joni at work there? Maybe she was.

The years passed. My daughter was a good pianist and she too was drawn to Joni's songs. She liked to play and sing but only when she was alone and in private, so I would often hear the strains of *Blue*. It was a huge pleasure, and remains so now.

In 2002 I visited California for the first time and suddenly realised that I would be at the actual birthplace of many of the songs I had listened to regularly for over twenty years. And so it was that in October, the day before I was due to return to England, I was walking along Zuma Beach watching the dolphins cruise along the tops of the waves when I stepped into a blob of tar and discovered the infuriating mess this can cause. As I tried to pick it off my toes, only to spread it onto my fingers, I could hear her shrill voice singing 'Carey' from the *Blue* album. She was ready to go to Europe, she sang, she was tired of having filthy fingernails and beach tar on her feet.

So there I stood on Zuma Beach, feeling (despite the tar) the most free and happy and complete that I had ever been in my entire life, and I could not help but say aloud so that any passing dolphin could hear 'OK Joni, I get it. The joke's on me. Thanks a lot!'

'New' 1970:
'I', 'we' and 'anyone else'

Helen Graham

The final sentence of an early *Shrew* magazine, which hit the streets of London in June 1970, states '(t)his *Shrew* is us' and asks ' . . . do we speak for anyone else?'[1] The politics of this question, naming an existing 'us' and opening it up to unnamed 'others', runs throughout the magazine's contributions. But it isn't only the imagined reader who goes unnamed. Of the twenty contributions, many of them first-person narratives, only two are attributed – the rest are deliberately anonymous.[2] Drawing on the troubled relationship between anonymity, personal accounts, the evoked 'us' and the desired 'anyone else', I want to attempt to respond to their question by asking how, only a matter of 12-18 months into the beginnings of the Women's Liberation Movement in Britain, did an exploration of identities shape the way *Shrew*'s writers thought about *doing* politics?

Shrew was originally produced in rotation by the different groups of the London Women's Liberation Workshop.[3] Unlike the *London Women's Liberation Workshop Newsletter*, which existed deliberately to communicate with women who already identified themselves with the politics of women's liberation, *Shrew* acted as the external publication of the London workshop (Setch 2001:26). In its conception, therefore, *Shrew*'s role was as a communicator. The June 1970 edition of *Shrew*, put together by the Tufnell Park group,[4] is enormously interesting for considering the identities of activists in the context of this desire to reach out beyond the existing mailing lists. The problems of the relationship between 'I', 'we' and 'anyone else', the individual, the collective and women as yet uninvolved, are explored through various contributions, from cartoons and poems to autobiographical reflections, and act as a linking theme throughout the magazine. In the final section, 'Bringing Home the Revolution', one of the contributors theorises this theme in terms of the magazine's form, commenting that '*Shrew* contains the contradiction that we have attempted to go beyond the academic forum of printing individual items, and have simultaneously rejected a collective policy statement'. This statement is crucial to the political energy which flows through *Shrew*. The writer is explicit about *Shrew*'s difficult balancing act: to take seriously individual voices without being individualistic while evoking collectivity between all women without assuming sameness.

Spaces between

The difficult 'balancing act' between the individual and collective is, as I have already indicated, mediated through concern surrounding the category of 'anyone else', of 'other' women. This sense of 'I'/'we' and 'us'/ 'anyone else' informs the prose poem of twenty four lines found on the second page of *Shrew*:

> I thought I'd found a total home in women's liberation. A space where I and all other women could meet, by definition. Words imprinted on my transparent body to be comprehended by those whose bodies are the same. But there's a different history flowing through that hair, those breasts.

The writer opens by evoking 'home', with all its resonances of safety, retreat and security. This dream of 'home', she cautions, is not to be found 'in' women's liberation as the 'different history' of 'other women' create what she later calls 'spaces' and 'chasm(s)' between her and them. Rather than simple retreat, the writer implies, the 'home' of women's liberation must carry domestic resonances as well. Women's liberation is a place for work, that of reading differences and deciphering their meaning.

These 'spaces' between women are made literal in one of the other accounts, which re-works the experience of being on an anti-Vietnam demonstration in London.[5] The *Shrew* writer describes a Saturday afternoon on an Oxford Street swarming with demonstrators.[6] Hundreds of people cried chants such as 'US Imperialism out' while hundreds of people doing their shopping looked on. For the writer, this split of pavement and street represented a 'chasm'. She held her placard facing outwards, towards the pavement, to try to make contact with some of the women who were waiting for buses or coming out of shops. Around her, 'men-of-some-left-wing-group' sneered, not joining in her chants of 'Women's Liberation = People's Liberation'. After a while she turned her placard back to the front, away from the women on the pavement. She describes how she felt, as she moved to face forward, as 'ashamed, really nervous inside, sensing betrayal, by me, of them, of me.' The writer locates her sense of betrayal in the unasked question about women and war, writing, 'I'm against the war. Of course. I'm a woman. What's the connection? The betrayal/betrayed welled up because we hadn't asked the question'. The Vietnam War is understood by the writer to be 'imperialist, racist, male chauvinist'. Yet no-one joined in the chants which attempted to make these links. Women-centred politics seemed not just to be ignored, but actively excluded. In such an atmosphere the street becomes, for the writer, an unavoidably gendered place. This creates the sense that there is an 'other world' of women with which she can't communicate, specifically because she is on the wrong side of the curb. For her, being a woman on the street – on the march rather than on the pavement – creates feelings of betrayal both of the women onlookers and of some notion of her female self.

The 'chasm' between women experienced by this writer is echoed by another autobiographical piece which reflects on being a non-mother taking a partner's child to school. Unlike the experience of the Vietnam demonstration, where it seemed impossible to communicate across the barrier between street and pavement, this second writer has temporary access, what she calls the 'key', to this 'other world'. For her this world is made up of 'women as mothers, but also women as shop assistants, teachers, grandmothers, big sisters' and she has gained access to it simply by having a child in tow. One afternoon she wanted to invite some of her partner's child's friends round for tea but realised, after she asked their parents, that although she seemed to have borrowed access to the 'key' she didn't actually 'know their language'. The 'key' allowed her to see in but not to fully integrate, making her ask '(a)nd how do we relate to a community where we don't (fully) possess a key?'

And on one side: the activist 'we'

The question raised on the final page of *Shrew*, 'do we speak for any-one else?', is central to all three accounts. Each writer is concerned that she is failing to form links with 'other' women, be they mothers or shoppers. The anxiety about lack of communication and lack of 'incommonness' circles around the writer's nagging awareness of them-selves, if not as feminists,[7] then as political activists, 'political women'. In the demonstration account the questions connecting women and war are not only forced on the writer by male resistance to feminist/women's

---

helen graham

anti-war intervention. They are also made plain through the discontinuity between street and pavement, between the labels earned through women's locations on different parts of Oxford Street, those of political woman (on the street) and non-political woman (on the pavement). In speaking of collective motivation for attending the demo, she recounts:

> We hardly talked to each other, as our brigade formed up. We had responded to overwhelming shock and frustration in the only form we knew, massing for a demonstration, playing out someone else's pattern and timetable as we flowed down the street past those hundreds of women.

Being a 'political woman', the writer suggests, means owning the identity, being prepared to be absorbed into the signifying practice of marching. 'Political woman' also means, at this point, in this context, dancing to another's tune, fitting into rituals of protest which are recognisable as rebellion and anger. These identities of the political woman, demo attendee, chanter and placard holder, seem increasingly impossible for the writer, not least because of the unsettling realisation that she had no influence over the logic of the demonstration or its consequences. Instead the process of being on the demo defined her against those women not protesting in a way that felt like betrayal. This concern over separation from 'other women' is seen by the writer at the school gates as being based on choice over fertility. She fears that the 'very choice (not to have a child) makes either ourselves or other women who are mothers exclude us from their world (and place us in) the business one of men'. For her this is a serious barrier to women's liberation, 'because it seems to legitimise us as women, this having physically borne a child, I wonder just in the political terms of women's liberation what ways it was possible to relate, to work, to organise, without the key to this world'. These writers, in different ways, express a worry that 'excluding ourselves' – going on demos rather than shopping and/or not having children – derives precisely from attempts to challenge the terms within which women function.

These concerns over activists' separation from 'other' women led to a deliberate attempt to de-fetishise political identity (as suggested in the cartoon labelled Figure One). In his article 'Identity and Cultural Studies: Is that all there is?' Lawrence Grossberg argues that political identity itself is an unhelpful concept. Instead he advocates, quoting Robert Young, what he calls 'singularity', a '"form of knowledge which respects the other without absorbing it into the same" or . . . the different' (1996:105), suggesting that activist communities might join together

162

'not by virtue of some common property which (is shared) . . . with all the other members of the set' but by '"belonging itself"' (Grossberg 1996:106). The writers in *Shrew* are grappling with these problematics: recognising difference without solidifying it as difference and creating a politics not based on activist identities but still evoking a 'we' that can reach out to 'anyone else'.

All together now: kaleidoscoping the 'we'

Shrew's writers' attempts to try to solve the problems of political identity all start with this core relationship, not just between 'us' and 'anyone else', but between 'I', 'we' and 'anyone else'. For the woman writing about the demonstration, this is most obvious. As she looks around the demo, feeling a sense of betrayal of the women shopping on Oxford Street, she realises that not asking questions about women and war, and the relationship between women and protesting against war, 'was the most apolitical thing I've done in a long time'. The prose poem also explores a relationship between the self and the other through the metaphor of searching:

163

> I am who am I. The other must find me. That's a lie, for
> the other is myself, that is whom I must find.
> [. . .]
> The Chasm is the same for both of us, that between what
> I say and what others hear, and that between the various
> components of the movement and the unknown millions
> of women who will perhaps never hear about it at all. To
> dance over one is to jump over the other, as we create
> ourselves and the Movement in a multiplicity of form.

The writer sets up the idea of a continuum, where liberation of self and other is not resident in either but is formed in the relationship between. Although mis-communication and lack of communication are seen as barriers, faith is placed in the processes of 'creation' and 'multiplicity' and a rejection of static modes of activism. This leads to a transformed 'we', one which by dancing, jumping and reinvention includes and therefore shifts as communication with 'other' women takes place. This lack of finality and emphasis on process is echoed in the final words of the magazine:

> There is no Women's Movement.

> We need a Women's Movement, but thinking that one
> existed, and that Shrew [sic] represented a part of it, was
> a mistake. Thinking that a movement exists makes women
> into another 'issue', a 'cause'. Like so many causes exter-
> nal to us, the women cause, totally engulfing us, provid-
> ing the illusion of a final solution. An imaginary move-
> ment can be as external to one's life as any old relation-
> ship with men. Making women a cause is degrading our-
> selves to the level of a demonstration tactic.

The desire for change, the writer argues, should not be seen as external to women's lives, but as an intrinsic part of it, emphasising change itself as indistinguishable from how you facilitate that change. Labelling women's liberation as another 'cause' is conceived of as reductionism, merely a tactic rather than the complete and radical overhaul of thinking, feeling and being aspired to by *Shrew*.

Shrew's writers, as I have shown, see possibility for change in the process of crossing spaces and of initiating communication. Communication with these 'other women', whether in the playground or on the demonstration, is, however, not reduced to a small step on a longer journey. Instead communication is conceived as an end in itself: the smallest gesture, like walking across and talking to another woman, has the potential, it seems, to collapse existing political and social certainties. This process of collapse works also for the activist 'we' that caused so much concern. If communication is successful, the writer suggests, there is hope that the 'we' will stretch to include 'other' women, becoming, therefore, something quite different. This belief in a kind of simultaneous process of change can be seen in the way in which *Shrew* as a magazine is thought about by the writer of the final section:

> Putting together Shrew has been an action for me. Our
> collective work on it has raised my consciousness of some
> of the problems of struggling with women. The end prod-
> uct is not just on paper, it is in my mind – in our minds. .
> [sic] It has been exciting and intense, the more so be-
> cause I felt no limitation of time and place.

Shrew's existence in this paragraph is both materially and temporally located and without 'limitation'. In practical terms the writer draws attention to the production of the magazine as something solid that can be read by others. However, she also focuses on the experience of producing *Shrew*, leaving them with ideas which seem so exciting that they have 'no limitation of time and space'. This balancing between the limited and unlimited nature of *Shrew* shows the distinctiveness of the politics formed in this edition. Here, as for the other writers, politics is conceived in terms of simultaneousness or, perhaps, as a kind of kaleidoscope, where the process of 'constantly' merging[8] now and future, location and limitlessness challenges the meaning of political change.

The politics of kaleidoscoping challenges enlightenment notions both of the constitution of the subject and what counts as change. In the *Shrew* accounts there is hope that there need not be a separation been the most particular action – speaking to others, learning the language of mothers – and the most general change. In short, attempts to work through the 'spaces' and talk, or make a connection with other women, has the potential to constitute change in itself. In this the politics developed in *Shrew* is very different to more familiar forms of politics such as 'building for' demonstrations or elections. 'Building for' events assumes there needs to be a step one, talking to people in order to convince them to attend and a step two, if enough people do it then change will take place either through lobbying or putting intense pressure on the establishment. *Shrew*'s politics collapses this logic.

While the quality of change may be different for different forms of politics there would seem to be only a fine line between kaleidoscopic politics and more traditional politics in terms of actually making them happen. Both still involve attempting to make connection with people (as yet) unfamiliar with your ideas. But while all politics may be better when done with a sense of excitement, *Shrew* suggests that it is precisely a sense of newness, a sense that this has not been tried before, that keeps the fine line in place. Kaleidoscoping can, *Shrew* implies, only happen when you absolutely believe it will work.

Just 'us': revising legacy

So, if you need to believe in newness to believe kaleidoscoping will work, what exactly does that mean for the slightly older and slightly more cynical feminism of 30 years on? Second wave feminism has constantly placed importance on legacy, fore-mothers, learning from and being inspired by the past.[9] Legacy, literally meaning something handed down, can be inspiring and useful – giving ideas that can be re-visioned as discussed at the Feminist Seventies Conference and suggested by Margaretta Jolly in this volume. But legacy or even re-vision, 'the act of looking back' (Rich 1979:35), we must recognise is not essential to 'good', exciting and successful politics. This lack of legacies sticks out in *Shrew*, there is simply no awareness of what came before. *Shrew* contains no referencing, no lip service to ideas of the left, only attempts to deal with the problems the group were facing. An historical approach to *Shrew* could emphasize the similarities with other forms of experimental politics but drawing these genealogies would miss the key political point – it doesn't appear to have felt like that to the writers, to them it was wholly new.[10]

In June last year, a few months after the Feminist Seventies Conference, I co-organised with York's Detached Youth Work Project a Young Women's Day called 'Big Sister', based on popular culture including the then omnipresent reality TV programme *Big Brother*. This day was financially possible because I had managed to get funding for 16-18 year olds to come to the conference but, and this taught me a few lessons, no young women had been interested. In the final session of the day we asked the participants if they had any idea what 'feminist' meant. There had been some concern amongst us organisers about this, expecting the familiar 'negative stereotypes' to come up. We were, however, very wrong. Some of the young women suggested a feminist was a very feminine woman, others agreed, but most said they didn't know. This, after all our angsting, was a bit of a revelation. While for the twenty-something youth work team feminism was clouded by a variety of meanings, for those under twenty the meanings were fading. Their responses made me realise that for many young women the stereotypes, the romanticism, the hurt, the recriminations, even the meaning of the most reductive definition of the word 'feminist' are gone.[11] This realisation could be a cause for bemoaning, for wondering where we went wrong, creating concern for a world where the power of feminism is forgotten. *Shrew* shows, however, that this absolutely does not have to be the case. As anyone who has ever attended an activist meeting will know, nothing kills radical politics like being told it has all been done before.

The young women were, for that day, our 'anyone else': 'other women'. As a very inexperienced youth worker I was in a similar position to the *Shrew* writers, I feared my inability to communicate, a factor which was marked not only by the difference between 'political woman' and the assumed category of 'non-political young woman' but also, as in *Shrew*, by class, accent and interests. To me, however, any attempt to breach the gaps and spaces by walking across the room did not, to say the least, feel like a kaleidoscope. It felt awkward, hugely difficult and constitutive of the spaces between us. One of the many reasons for my awkwardness was my assumption that the young women had pre-existing negative ideas about feminism, a concern *Shrew*'s writers just didn't seem to have. When we discovered the young women had no preconceptions at all about feminism we were suddenly and surprisingly in precisely the same position as *Shrew*'s activists. The young women had big questions about the world, about sex, STDs, jobs and about the unfairness they experienced. This was a reminder of the importance of feminist ideas – at their most effective they can offer a way of seeing the world which stops women understanding their experiences as isolated events. What was so exciting about the Young Women's Day is that never having heard of 'feminism' not only didn't stop the participants talking about their lives but in some ways helped them in developing a mutual way of seeing things which connected each of them as women.

The discussion between the young women only took place in the form it did because 'we', the organisers, were women who believed that getting young women together on their own was important. One of *Shrew*'s anxieties is about precisely this desire to 'reach out'. The activist 'we', *Shrew* suggests, has to be prepared to 'start something', make contact, organise something, but it also needs to be prepared to be transformed by the 'other women'. When I argue for newness, it is not, therefore, about not having a pre-existing feminist 'we', nor is it about being young or about forgetting the past – it is about not getting bogged down and losing what makes politics effective. Feminist politics should be about analysing and changing the world and, as in *Shrew*, the process is all: who put up the posters should become irrelevant.

167

'Do "we" speak for anyone else?'

There are two unanswered questions which echo around *Shrew*'s articulated one: who speaks and how can that 'we' both exist as a basis for politics and be ready to be transformed? In *Shrew*, this anxiety – about the relationship between 'I', 'we' and 'anyone else' – led to thinking about ways of transforming the existing 'we' of women's liberation. In doing so they developed, I argue, a kind of kaleidoscopic politics, a politics which only maintains its potency while new, fresh, exciting and believed in. We could learn from this, but equally we could forget it – the feeling of newness that enabled *Shrew*'s ideas suggests we could do a lot worse than reinventing and creating new wheels. We need to recognise that the meaning of 'feminism' is open – it is losing its daily currency, becoming an empty word that could be filled with a similar sense of newness and energy as in June 1970. Or we could, of course, create new words with different meanings to perform different political aims. Re-invoking the legacy of newness and jettisoning the legacy of 'tried and failed' might just mean that 'we' – in this instance people who already believe in collective change – can also ask, 'Do we, now, today, speak for anyone else?' We have nothing to lose but our 'we'.

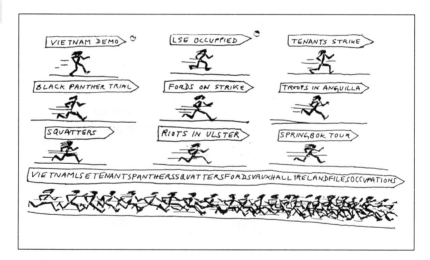

Figure One:

The identity of 'political woman' displayed in the demo account is sent up by another cartoon in the magazine. Here the running from protest to protest led them to be all melded together showing, I think, both the interconnectedness of all the causes from Vietnam to a tenants strike and also the stress and guilt which having firm political beliefs can entail.

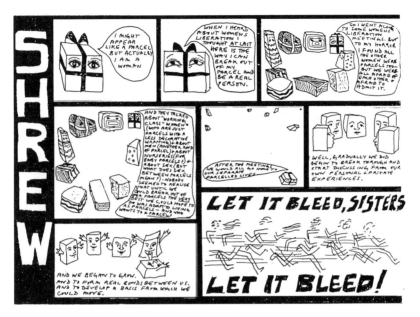

Figure Two:

This slightly disturbing image throws up many questions. Is the image of a parcel chosen because the wrapping can be peeled off to reveal a pre-existing, pre-social 'true' woman? Or is it not about unwrapping but rather morphing, not about any true womanhood but about possibilities for new ways of being a woman? Either way, talking and creating real bonds between women is believed to create a shift so that movement, in both senses, can begin.

169

Notes

1 *Shrew* did not have page numbers. For full reference details see bibliography.

2 The named women, Sue Cowley and Chris Filmer, are only named because they were acting as contacts for two childcare initiatives the group wanted to start. It would be possible to track down from later editions of *Shrew* the names of women who were in the group which produced this magazine. However, as there were specific political reasons for this anonymity I am more interested in their reasons for anonymity rather than diffusing their decision 30 years on by guessing.

3 By the time of the last issue which came out in 1977 *Shrew* had gone

nationwide and was being written by women's groups around the country (Bouchier 1983:100).

4 This edition of *Shrew* was written by the 'new' Tufnell Park group, the old one having recently disbanded (see contribution to *Shrew*, June 1970, 'Rambling Notes'). Although the name of the new group was decided the day before they finished *Shrew*, as stated in the final contribution 'Bringing the Revolution Back Home', it is not actually given at any point in the publication.

5 This demonstration was specifically against Nixon's decision in 1970 to officially enter Cambodia. The US government believed the Vietcong was supplying their troops through Cambodia (Hawkins 1968:173n). The US had already used Napalm in Cambodia (Heineman 1994:157) even before this official announcement but had initially lied about pre-1970 military attacks on Cambodia because they were illegal under international law (Hawkins 1968:173).

6 Oxford Street is a famous shopping area in central London.

7 At different points in the seventies 'feminist' had different resonances. In oral histories I have collected for my PhD research it has become clear that 'feminist' in the early 70s had connotations of liberal feminism. There was also a sense that 'feminist' harked back to early 20th century campaigns and that the WLM was doing something completely different (Sebestyen 1979). *Shrew* is, however, clearly in the process of grappling with some kind of 'feminist' or 'women-centred consciousness'.

8 *The Concise Oxford English Dictionary* defines Kaleidoscope as '1) a tube containing mirrors and pieces of coloured glass or paper, whose reflections produce changing patterns when the tube is rotated 2) a constantly changing group of bright or interesting objects' (1990:644). It is the sense of constantly changing and constantly merging that I want to focus on in my use of kaleidoscope.

9 To take examples from a range of sources: *Shrew* (1972?) 'East End Women' 4,4; Dale Spender (1983) *There's Always Been A Women's Movement This Century* London: Pandora; *Trouble and Strife* 'Writing our own history', Vol 1, 1983 and 2, 1984; Lesbian History Group (1989) *Not a Passing Phase: Reclaiming Lesbians in History 1840-1985* London: The Women's Press; Jill Radford (1994) 'History of Women's Liberation Movements in Britain: A Reflective Personal History', in Gabriele Griffin et al (eds) *Stirring it: Challenges for Feminism* London: Taylor and Francis.

10 Sheila Rowbotham has noted this sense of newness in relation to the WLM. She writes '(d)espite feminist interest in women's history, we have not referred what we are doing much to past traditions of revolutionary organization. . . . In

this way the women's movement has shared with libertarian Marxism a sense of beginning anew' (1980:43).

11 The young women were from a very specific educational and class background. None of them were doing AS or A-Levels, they were doing either vocational training, had jobs or were full time mothers. While the looks of complete blankness may not be found on the faces of A-level students who in some form have 'studied' feminism, the reactions of the young women at the Big Sister day do, however, say something about the fading circulation of 'feminism' in general knowledge.

Bibliography:

Shrew (1970) no title, June.

Shrew (1972?) 'East End Women' 4,4.

Trouble and Strife (1984, 1985) 'Writing our own history', 3 - 5.

Allen, R. E. (1990) *The Concise Oxford English Dictionary of Current English* Oxford: Clarendon Press.

Bouchier, David (1983) *The Feminist Challenge: The Movement for Women's Liberation in Britain and the USA* London: Macmillan Press.

Grossberg, Lawrence (1996) 'Identity and Cultural Studies: Is That All There Is?', in Stuart Hall and Paul du Gay (eds) *Questions of Cultural Identity* London: Sage.

Hawkins, Elliot D. (1968) 'An Approach to Issues of International Law Raised by United States Action in Vietnam', in Richard A. Falk (ed) *Vietnam and International Law* Princeton: Princeton University Press.

Heineman, Kenneth J. (1994) *Campus Wars: The Peace Movement of American State Universities in the Vietnam Era* New York: New York University Press.

Lesbian History Group (1989) *Not a Passing Phase: Reclaiming Lesbians in History 1840-1985* London: The Women's Press.

helen graham

Radford, Jill (1994) 'History of Women's Liberation Movements in Britain: A Reflective Personal History', in Gabriele Griffin, Marianne Hester, Shrin Rai and Sasha Roseneil (eds) *Stirring it: Challenges for Feminism* London: Taylor and Francis.

Rowbotham, Sheila, Lynne Segal and Hilary Wainwright (1980) *Beyond the Fragments: Feminism and the Making of Socialism* London: Merlin Press.

Sebestyen, Amanda (1979) 'Tendencies in the Movement: Then and Now', *Feminist Practice: Notes from the 10th Year* London: In Theory Press.

Setch, Eve Grace (2001) *The Women's Liberation Movement in Britain 1969-1979: Organisation, Creativity and Debate* Unpublished Thesis, University of London.

Spender, Dale (1983) *There's Always Been A Women's Movement this Century* London: Pandora.

After the Seventies:

Greenham Common Women and Dreams of a Common Language

Margaretta Jolly

I

Twenty years after the founding of one of the
most idealistic and long-running feminist anti-militarist campaigns, it
is a good time to reflect on the Greenham Common Women's Peace
Camp. Although the protests at Greenham Common Royal Airforce base
were a movement of the 1980s, their controversial crossing of existing
feminist and pacifist alignments shed light on the politics of gender,
motherhood and the military that preceded them. Associated both with
apolitical mothers fearful for their children's lives and with radical
feminism, the campaign also drew on a less obvious heritage of liberal
feminism that was, in my view, important to the camp's later success.
Drawing in thousands more women than nearly any other feminist
campaign in Britain at the time, it unexpectedly answered some of the
needs of seventies feminists as well as providing a way into feminism
for many others, eventually becoming far more radical than its original
design. Ironically, anti-nuclear activity provided a holding point for a
fast-dividing women's movement while looking forward to its more
diverse political future.[1]

How did the Greenham Common Women's Peace Camp begin? To
many it seemed mad, unprecedented, risky. Established on 5 September
1981, the camp was the surprise culmination of a walk for peace organised
by Wales-based activists Ann Pettitt, Carmen Cuttler, Lynne Whittemore
and Liney Seward. Calling themselves Women for Life on Earth, the
thirty-six women, four men and a few children delivered, on arrival at

Greenham Common, Berkshire, a letter to the Base Commandant stating their case against plans to site nuclear missiles in Britain. 'We are a group of women from all over Britain who have walked one hundred and twenty miles from Cardiff to deliver this letter to you', it began, continuing:

> Some of us have brought our babies with us this entire distance. We fear for the future of all our children, and for the future of the living world which is the basis of all life. We have undertaken this action because we believe that the nuclear arms race constitutes the greatest threat ever faced by the human race and our living planet. We have chosen Greenham Common as our destination because it is this base which our Government has chosen for 96 'Cruise' [missiles] without our consent.
>
> (Hopkins and Harford 1984:16)[2]

The Commandant's indifferent response was to invite them to stay as long as they wanted. Fateful words! The siting of 'Cruise' turned out to be a mass wake-up call to the realities behind Cold War threats. In December 1979 NATO had decided that it would deploy 572 new American nuclear missiles, 108 Pershing II ballistic missiles and 464 Tomahawk ground-launched cruise missiles in Western Europe (Smith 1980:110). This was ostensibly to match the development of Soviet SS20s. Both sets of weapons were designed to preempt each other with 'first strike' capacity and their siting in Europe suggested superpower plans for a 'limited' nuclear war in the territory between them. Despite this, Britain, with some other European governments, agreed to host the missiles, though they were to remain entirely under US control. Two weeks after NATO's decision, the USSR invaded Afghanistan and in response President Carter halted ongoing Strategic Arms Limitation Talks from the Senate. Thatcher had just been elected, Reagan came in during 1980, and the political climate could not have been worse. It was a September the 11th that seemed likely to go on for months and years.

Women for Life on Earth thus walked on the cusp of a dramatically reviving peace consciousness: Europe for Nuclear Disarmament and the World Disarmament Campaign had been launched in 1980; national membership of CND jumped from 3,000 in 1981 to 50,000 in 1983; demonstrations of a quarter of a million or more filled Rome, Amsterdam, Paris, Madrid, Helsinki and London in October 1981, with more than half a million in New York the following June (Jones 1983:2). But the camp quickly became the darling of the peace movement for its media-grabbing women-led direct action (Young 1990). The small walking party had initially got almost no press interest but when four women chained themselves to the fence, suffragette-style, and began to develop their distinctive 'embrace the base' actions, the media, military and government certainly did take notice. The articulation of anti-militarism through women's interests was fresh after a decade where most western pacifism was absorbed in men as soldiers or conscientious objectors to the Vietnam War. The Greenham camp and its creative style offered the peace movement a new focus and perspective, and activists a different kind of outlet for their fears.

The romance between anti-nukes and feminists didn't last. Led by media smears, the peace movement began to see the 'gender' issue as 'distracting' from the peace one, and the 'lifestyles' of the campers as having taken over the spotlight. The Campaign for Nuclear Disarmament indeed commissioned a report in 1983 on public perceptions of the camp (Roseneil 2000:157-158). But the anxieties of mainstream peace groups gauge how significant Greenham became as a feminist event, perhaps indeed a candidate for the most successful populariser of ideas of 1970s feminism in Britain. Sasha Roseneil proposes feminism, anarchism, socialism and pacifism as four interrelated heritages of resistance behind Greenham (Roseneil 2000). As she charmingly puts it, these functioned as 'Grandmothers, Aunts and Older Cousins' in protestors' appeals to witches of the fifteenth-seventeenth centuries, songs of English Civil War Diggers, direct actions and street theatre from Suffragettes to Aldermastoners, anti-Vietnamers and Situationists. But the 'Big Sister' to the camp was obviously the Second Wave women's movement. The campers early on decided to go women-only, albeit against the wishes of some women and men, arguing that the male walkers dominated, were more easily violent in demonstrations, didn't do the housework and broke down community solidarity. This nascent separatism became full blown within a year, as more explicitly feminist women joined the camp. Roseneil's sketch of British feminism in 1981 suggests that Greenham appeared just when the movement was both powerful and in need of a newly unifying cause:

175

> For the women involved in the movement in Britain its first decade was a heady time of intense organising and life-changing experiences. By the early 1980s the heat of the early years of the movement had lessened and a process of institutionalisation had begun. The annual national women's liberation conferences were a thing of the past, largely because the movement had become so large and diverse, but there were national networks of locally based

feminist groups and services, such as rape crisis centres, lesbian lines and women's refuges. Many cities had their own newsletters and women's centres, and there were a number of well-established national feminist newsletters and magazines, such as *Spare Rib* and *Outwrite*. Strong friendship networks existed and there were thousands of communal women's households around the country. Predominantly the creation of lesbian feminists, there was also a thriving feminist culture based around women-only discos, women's bands and theatre companies, and a growing literature of feminist novels, poetry and plays published by a small number of women's publishing houses. The social networks, political spaces and ideas of the women's liberation movement made Greenham possible.
(Roseneil 2000:32-33)

Indeed for many, Greenham was the discovery of those networks, spaces and ideas. Again and again, women who went to Greenham as pacifists rather than feminists testified to the transformative effect of experiencing public, women-only action. As a sit-in became a feminist way of life, the camp's politics became ever more encompassing and idealistic, debating issues such as animal rights and nuclear testing in the Pacific – though race became a subject for internal division in the process. (This holism was in direct contrast to the rest of the peace movement, whose strategy, now it had mainstream backing, was to narrow its initially sweeping aims to the removal of Cruise and Pershing.) In Roseneil's words, Greenham thus departed from the 'straighter feminisms . . . concerned with achieving rights for women' in favour of 'a cultural politics of opening up and reconfiguring what it means be a woman' (Roseneil 2000:4). A crucial part of this was its lesbian dynamic as 'a social world in which relations with other women were central' and 'assumptions about men's and women's complementarity, and practices of female dependency, hesitancy and quiescence were challenged' (Roseneil 2000:6).

So Greenham brilliantly put together 1970s feminism with 1980s anti-nuclearism in a way that for at least two years gained mainstream coverage and appeal for what were some of the women's movement's most radical ideas. But if Greenham's political relationship to 1970s movements was one of little sister to big sister, this was a more complicated and sometimes adversarial relationship than romances with great grandmothers and aunts long dead. Although one of the cherished principles of Greenham was its diversity and the principle of letting each woman speak for herself, I wish to explore that political relationship through one individual's story, that of Ann Pettitt, a central public relations officer for Greenham's first couple of months as well as the initiator of the Women for Life on Earth walk. This is not to elevate Pettitt's contribution above others, nor to pretend that Pettitt was representative, but Pettitt's political history is especially revealing of the connections between 1970s and 1980s feminisms. It should also be said that Pettitt has given her papers to the Glamorgan County Records Office and so her story is more accessible than most.

II

In 1981 Ann Pettitt was a feminist as well as an anti-militarist and environmentalist. Although she largely networked for the walk with CND, she also had connections to Women Against the Nuclear Threat, established in 1980, and the American ecofeminist group Women and Life on Earth. Moreover, she had been involved in early women's lib debates in London before moving to her smallholding in Wales. Her early publicity explained the march as 'women-led' for several reasons: because women's role as carers means we have not had the power, nor probably the wish, to perpetuate the nuclear arms race; because it is women who bear the weight of cuts in public expenditure when money goes to the military, and because women are more vulnerable to radiation when pregnant. In a speech to a mixed peace meeting in West Wales in July 1981, she anticipated the question 'Why women?' with:

> It seems appropriate, that's all. I don't want to labour these points, but I can't help but observe to myself that ideas such as 'Theatre Nuclear War' whereby an entire densely populated continent is sacrificed in order to save the two antagonists in a war, are cooked up and rehearsed and given credibility and even respectability in the collective mind of a virtually exclusive male military and political establishment, not one member of whom, I could safely guess, has ever performed a simple humanising task such as changing a nappy in his life.[3]

Pettitt pragmatically refused 'to labour' the underlying feminist interest in her argument, but this ironic alignment of men with a destructive 'cooking' on the one hand and mothers with truer public work on the other has radical tones. These also emerge in her interest in the nascent ecofeminist movement, naming the original march 'Women for Life on

Earth' after the American group Women and Life on Earth with whom it later merged. But these more visionary aspects of the gender politics of war went alongside a deep ambivalence about what she felt was the women's movement's mistaken and increasing emphasis on sexuality as the site of patriarchal oppression and its consequent moralism about sex.

In 1980, Pettitt sent an article stating as much to the national women's lib paper *Spare Rib,* ironically headed 'Feminism for her own Good'. This caused such a furore amongst the staff that they published an editorial explaining why they couldn't print it and inviting members to come to an open debate on 'controversial issues' (Editorial and 'Letters Extra' 1980: cover page; 40-41). Some felt that there was an anti-lesbian flavour in her complaints, further fanned when Pettitt succeeded in getting the article printed in the more mainstream and straight *Guardian* women's page (Pettitt 1980). Pettitt was also one of those whose responses to the Leeds Revolutionary Feminists' notorious 1979 paper on political lesbianism was published in the national feminist newsletter *WIRES* and reprinted in *Love Your Enemy: The Debate Between Heterosexual Feminism and Political Lesbianism.* In the same year that she was tirelessly gathering support for the walk to Greenham, she wrote:

178

> Surely the Leeds Revolutionary Feminist Group Paper, 'Political Lesbianism' clearly and directly contravenes the demand for the right to a self defined sexuality. It is also the most patronising, arrogant piece of rubbish I have ever read, including orthodox psychology etc about women.
> . . . Yours in no sisterhood whatsoever, Ann Pettitt.
>
> (Onlywomen Press 1981:14)

In some ways, Pettitt can be seen as a liberal feminist who had become disillusioned with the women's movement and anyway, by 1981, felt the nuclear threat was more important than all others. But Pettitt's correspondence suggests that from the start she saw women's peace activism as a correction not only to the peace movement but to the *women's* movement, essentially redirecting feminist sympathies towards the lot of (heterosexual) mothers. This went further than classic liberal humanist feminism, which has historically positioned motherhood as incompatible with women's need to succeed in the public sphere. Rather, it entwined humanism with the socialist feminist case that it was women's poverty and social exclusion (especially in mothering) not sexuality that was the root of their oppression. This materialist analysis was further interwoven with the holistic ethic of care for the planet proposed by ecofeminism. In 1991, on the occasion of Greenham's tenth anniversary, she wrote:

> While the feminism of the seventies, emphasizing equal-
> ity with men, had evaded areas of difference such as moth-
> erhood, Greenham shifted the debate to the relative val-
> ues of male and female cultures. Many women who re-
> sponded to Greenham found a new solidarity and a pride
> in motherhood: we care, we are responsible, because we
> have the babies. (Pettitt 1991)

What is the significance of this for Greenham as a whole? Although
Pettitt was of course only one individual and one link between the
women's movement of the 1970s and Greenham, I propose that her
story is symptomatic of the complex political culture behind the camp's
initial widespread appeal to women. Controversially set against various
women's lib orthodoxies though her views were at that time, particularly
in their suspicion of lesbian feminism, they were nevertheless deeply
indebted to seventies' politicisation of mothering. It is less surprising
then that the traditional terms of caring for their unborn children, the
planet, and others associated with the women's peace movement turned
out to be so quickly compatible with a stronger feminism, despite many
feminists' initial doubts. It is significant that the 'faint-hearted feminist'
Martha, the protagonist of Jill Tweedie's popular *Guardian* column of
that time, was finally able to be fully in agreement with her separatist
alter ego Mary over the Greenham protests. In her weekly 'letter from
Martha', Tweedie, as editor of *The Guardian's* women's page (who had
printed Pettitt's protest against feminist moralising), generally begged
sympathy for educated and opinionated women who nevertheless
accepted a bored and restless lot as unpaid wives and mothers. But
when Martha and her sexist civil servant husband Josh spy Mary in the
television coverage of the 12 December 1982 'Embrace the Base' action,
hanging baby clothes on the military fence, Martha feels Mary has got
things 'into proportion', while she is merely minding the kids back home.
Josh, spluttering at his exclusion from women-only action, accuses Mary
of stealing the clothes from an Oxfam shop: she 'wouldn't know a human
infant from a Sainsbury's Christmas cracker until [she] pulled it and no
funny hats fell out' (Tweedie 1983:86, 104). Tweedie's point was that
'many housewives were overlooked in the explosive beginnings of the
Women's Movement', that 'no one fights for what is, only for what
might be' (Tweedie 1983:4). Against the odds, Greenham seemed to
move between both.

Greenham's odd union of feminisms, tempting the 'fainthearted'
to a much stronger stance, shows more than the strategic importance
of a mother-friendly cause. Just as key was its women-only policy.

margaretta jolly

Living outdoors in a women-led and then women-only community, next to a largely men-only military base, even for only a few days, for many proved the conduit to feminism of a visceral kind. And here Pettitt's argument that sexuality was the wrong target proved dramatically misplaced. The stark visibility of the patriarchal dimensions of the military only seemed to support women's intuitive sense that sexuality and gender separatism *did* indeed have some bearing on the Cold War and on the policing of and locals' responses to the camp. Thus the camp's 'ethic of care' was both sexualised and spiritualised in women's sense of physical connection to each other and to the earth rather than to men or even children. Alongside the community of younger lesbians without dependents that Roseneil's study emphasises, a significant number of mothers came, stayed, and sometimes came out.

What made this particularly impressive was its expression by women across class and age, if not ethnicity. Of course, the key material condition of this was that women were judged legally entitled to claim dole from Greenham, making it possible to live there without savings or a job. And it is crucial to state that Greenham was of all campaigns a diverse and leaderless one, made by women of vastly different backgrounds and outlooks. Its famous 'rainbow of gates', each camp representing a particular taste and community, represented this graphically. But overall, it was the prominence of both sexuality and spirituality that distinguished its feminism as much as its peace politics, whether it was walking widdershins around the camp, constructing a 'love bender',[4] running self defense workshops against sexual harassment by local men, or hanging tampons on the fence (Young 1990; Starhawk 1990:248-252).

Many Big Sister liberal feminists were dismayed at this turn, most notably Pettitt herself. Pettitt, with nine others, sent a circular letter proposing that men as well as women attend the 10 December 1983 demonstration and later questioned the camp's direction in several national papers.[5] Other seventies' feminists worried for different reasons. Onlywomen Press critiqued Greenham from a radicalesbian perspective as glorifying women's traditional self sacrifice (Onlywomen Press 1983), socialist feminists like Lynne Segal worried about its essentialism (Segal 1987), and black/working-class feminists argued that unless peace-activists recognised the underlying economic and racist-imperialist issues that drove the arms race, disarmament would remain solely a white middle-class issue (Brown 1990).[6] (Yet Wages for Housework, also dedicated to an economic, anti-racist critique of women's oppression, still saw it worth their while to take over a camp at Greenham's main gate.[7]) Despite disagreements, in the context of the bitter self-criticism opening up in the fragmenting women's movement as a whole, Greenham in its heyday must be judged both as enormously unifying and as a link between private and public in the best seventies tradition.

III

Yet what legacy has Greenham left the peace movement today? The INF (Intermediate Nuclear Forces) Treaty, signed by Presidents Reagan and Gorbachev on 8 December 1987, announced the process of nuclear detente and a dramatic reduction in military spending that amongst many positive results saw Cruise leave Greenham from 1989 and the base return to common land in 2000. But today there are at least 24,000 nuclear warheads still in existence worldwide and the number of countries possessing nuclear weapons is increasing. The terrorist attack on New York on 11 September 2001 has fuelled President Bush's determination to relaunch the so-called U.S. National Missile Defense 'Son of Star-Wars' system, part of which is to be sited at the US Department Of Defense National Security Agency Station at Menwith Hill in Yorkshire. The long-time women's camp at this base and at Aldermaston are heroically continuing Greenham-style actions of creative protest that link peace to feminism. But, in general, it might appear that the peace movement today (such as the current Stop the War campaign[8]) hardly features their kind of links with feminism. While the European peace movement itself has had to regroup since the Cold War, this is certainly in part because the British women's movement itself is no longer as obviously visible. Natasha Walter, one prominent face of what the media proposes as Third Wave feminism, writes of 'dungareed' Greenham as having been 'double-edged' for women, – these days anyway feminists can be 'insiders' as well as 'outsiders' (Walter 1999:172). Even road protestor activist Kate Evans writes of Greenham as a 'funky' heritage rather than as a model for going women-only (Evans 1998:151). A recent editorial in an edition of *Peace News* devoted to 'gender and militarism' opens by expecting the reader's 'big yawn. Are they trotting out those banale "sex differences" again?' (Cockburn 2001:10). Meanwhile, memories of Greenham continue to reflect the political differences in its origins. I went to a commemorative reunion for the beginning of the Women for Life on Earth walk in Cardiff in August 2001 and was surprised at the virtual silence of any mention of feminism let alone lesbianism – straight CND was the order of the day. In parallel, a reunion for campers at what is now Greenham Common reflected the lesbian-centred community of the later years. Three months later I again attended a

181

commemoration of Greenham at the Welsh Women's Archive day, this a women's event at which Sasha Roseneil was the guest speaker. Roseneil's cheery celebration of Greenham's 'queer' garnered a largely thoughtful silence.

Yet it would be a serious mistake to conclude that there is no fruitful intersection between feminism and anti-militarism today, nor that Greenham didn't have at least an indirect influence. It is rather that, as with the rest of women's liberation, 'the problem is not the death or the end of feminism but, rather, coming to terms with the fact that its political, strategic, and interpretive power has been so great as to produce innumerable modes of doing – whether activist, practical, theoretical, or just "quiet" – that have moved well beyond the mother term, already fractured at its origin' (Bronfen and Kavka 2001:xi). In the diffuse globalisation of war and terrorism today, we find an equally globalised plethora of gender-informed peace groups that very often also have a Greenham-like belief in personal change. This ranges from Cypriot, Irish and Bosnia-Herzegovina women challenging partition lines; to New Profile, 'a feminist movement of women, men and youth, working together to civil-ize Israeli culture' through supporting Israeli conscientious objectors; to the non-violent Women's Action group at

the anti-globalisation protests; to lobbyists behind the first UN resolution on women, peace and security, and the now high-profile work of the women-only Women in Black.[9] Anu Pillay describes the mission of the African Women's Anti-War Coalition in South Africa in terms that move confidently between women's separatism and integration:

> These women [peace negotiators and mediators] will work towards combining the masculine and feminine ideals towards an integrated approach to conflict management rather than the one-sided masculine, patriarchal strategies that consistently emerge from these institutions and structures. At this point, the Coalition prefers to be a women-only institution to avoid the inevitable power struggles and diffusion of foci that would result if men were present. However, this is not to say that like-minded men will not be welcomed in the future once the coalition has established itself as a strong force to be reckoned with in terms of gender transformation. (Pillay 2001)

In the genealogy of today's resistance movements, Greenham can certainly be counted as an aunt, a cousin, and for some very definitely the 'big sister'. Rather than looking for a common language, we can be glad there is a multi-lingual conversation in which women are still dreaming.

Notes

1 I would like to thank Niamh Moore and Jay Prosser for stimulating discussions in the writing of this article, Ann Pettitt for her generosity and interest in sharing her materials, Sasha Roseneil for her encouragement and Susan Edwards at the Glamorgan Record Office for her care in archival guidance.

2 Letter writing was an important symbolic as well as pragmatic element of the campaign. See my article 'Writing the Web: Letters from the Women's Peace Movement' in *The Feminist Seventies* web book. <www.feminist-seventies.net/greenham.html>

3 Typescript of the speech in Glamorgan Record Office, GB 214 D/WLE 2/1.

4 Benders were temporary shelters constructed out of saplings or dead wood, and plastic. One that was hidden in some bushes was a place for lovers to use.

5 This circular and letters responding to it are held in the Glamorgan Record Office. Reference GB 214 DWLE/6/11.

6 See also the section 'No Nukes' in Kanter, Lefanu, Shah and Spedding (1984). This includes a letter by L.B. to *Lysistrata*; the Brighton Women's Liberation peace movement letter, proposing heterosexual women strike on sex with men as a peace protest; an 'Open Letter to Women in WONT and the Women's Peace Alliance' by Sophie Laws arguing against the Greenham protest and a reply by Lesley West. Hall Carpenter Archives and Lesbian Oral History Group's *Inventing Ourselves* (1989) includes several testimonies of Greenham's role in coming out, but also its association with white (racist) women.

7 See Junor and Howse (1995) for an account of the camp from the perspective of women allied to Wages for Housework that emphasises its later years. Roseneil (2000) analyses the history of this group at the camp as the most important of Greenham's inner political divisions.

8 This campaign began as a response to the United States' bombing of Afghanistan subsequent to terrorist attacks on Manhattan, 11 September 2001. The campaign is a coalition including the British Campaign for Nuclear Disarmament and The Muslim Association of Great Britain. At the time of writing (Spring 2003) it is currently campaigning to stop the US invasion of Iraq and its general 'war on terrorism' and to stand against that war's racist backlash and erosion of civil rights.

9 On 31 October 2000 the UN Security Council adopted Resolution 1325 that called for the prosecution of crimes against women; increased protection of women and girls during war; more women to be appointed to UN peacekeeping

operations and field missions and more women in the decision-making process at all levels. Women in Black, begun in 1988 by Israeli, Palestinian and American women protesting non-violently against the treatment of Palestinians, now encompasses such groups as Women in Black Belgrade and an English branch which in the 1999 Kosovan war entered the Fairford airbase to prevent US planes from taking off on bombing missions. Currently (Spring 2003) the New York branch has been protesting for a peaceful response to the terrorist bombings in the US and against the bombing of Iraq.

Bibliography

Unpublished letters cited are in the Glamorgan Record Office. I am extremely grateful for permission to use them.

Blackwood, Caroline (1984) *On the Perimeter* London: Heinemann.

184 Bronfen, Elizabeth and Misha Kavka (eds) (2001) *Feminist Consequences: Theory for the New Century* New York: Columbia University Press.

Brown, Wilmette (1990) *Black Women and the Peace Movement* Bristol: Falling Wall Press.

Cambridge Women's Peace Collective (ed) (1984) *My Country is the Whole World: An Anthology of Women's Work on Peace and War* London: Pandora.

Cockburn, Cynthia (ed) (2001) *Peace News: Gender and Militarism* 2443, June-August.

Cook, Alice and Gwyn Kirk (1983) *Greenham Women Everywhere: Dreams, Ideas, and Actions from the Women's Peace Movement* London: Pluto Press.

Evans, Kate (1998) *Copse: A Cartoon Book of Tree Protesting* Biddestone, Wilts: Orange Dog Productions.

Hall Carpenter Archives and Lesbian Oral History Group (eds) (1989) *Inventing Ourselves: Lesbian Life Stories* London: Routledge.

Hopkins, Sarah and Barbara Harford (1984) *Greenham Common: Women at the Wire* London: Women's Press.

Jones, Lynne (1983) *Keeping the Peace* London: The Women's Press.

Junor, Beth and Katrina Howse (1995) *Greenham Common Women's Peace Camp: A History of Non-violent Resistance, 1984-1995* London: Working Press.

Kanter, Hannah, Sarah Lefanu, Shaila Shah and Carole Spedding (eds) (1984) *Sweeping Statements: Writings from the Women's Liberation Movement 1981-83* London: The Women's Press.

Lelland, Stephanie (1983) 'Greenham Women Are Everywhere', in Joy Holland (ed) *Feminist Action I* London: Battle Axe Books.

Onlywomen Press (eds) (1981) *Love Your Enemy? The Debate Between Heterosexual Feminism and Political Lesbianism* London: Onlywomen Press.

Onlywomen Press (eds) (1983) *Breaching the Peace* London: Onlywomen Press.

Pettitt, Ann (1980) 'Can A World Change Without Men and Women Changing It Together?', *The Guardian* exact date unknown:8.

Pettitt, Ann (1983) 'Letter to My Neighbour', in Dorothy Thompson (ed) *Over Our Dead Bodies: Women Against the Bomb* London: Virago.

Pettitt, Ann (1991) 'Women: War and Pieces - On the 10th anniversary of the first marches to Greenham Common airbase, Ann Pettitt, one of the organisers, sums up the movement's achievements', *The Guardian* 3 September:33.

Pillay, Anu (2001) 'The African Women's Anti-War Coalition', *Peace News: Gender and Militarism* 2443, June-August.

Roseneil, Sasha (1995) *Disarming Patriarchy: Feminism and Political Action at Greenham* Buckingham; Philadelphia: Open University Press.

Roseneil, Sasha (2000) *Common Women, Uncommon Practices: The Queer Feminisms of Greenham* London; New York: Cassell.

Segal, Lynne (1987) *Is the Future Female? Troubled Thoughts on Contemporary Feminism* London: Virago.

Smith, Dan (1980) 'The European Nuclear Theatre', in E.P. Thompson and Dan Smith (eds) *Protest and Survive* Harmondsworth: Penguin.

Spare Rib (1980) 'Editorial' and 'Letters Extra', Issue 98, September:Inside Cover and 40-1.

Starhawk (1990) *Truth or Dare: Encounters with Power, Authority, and Mystery* San Francisco: HarperCollins.

Tweedie, Jill (1983) *More from Martha: Further Letters from a Fainthearted Feminist* London: Robson.

Walter, Natasha (1999) *The New Feminism* London: Virago.

Young, Alison (1990) *Femininity in Dissent* London: Routledge.

contributors

Josephine Brain is a PhD student at London School of Economic's Gender Institute.

Sarah Cheverton completed an MSc in Social Research methods (2002) and is currently volunteering for WOMANKIND, an international women's rights organisation. An ardent feminist since age 11, when she discovered the suffragettes, Sarah aims to write/research on international women's rights, and feels a strong, if nostalgic affiliation with the seventies Women's Liberation Movement.

Hyung-Mee Choi was born to a couple who lost their family during the Korean War. Raised in the poorest area of Seoul. Married with two kids. During her Master's study at the University of York she realised how complicated oppressive structures can be. Now working as a pastor.

Hilary Doran, a country kid from Montana, went to college in Kansas and spent 5 years in Guatemala working with women's cooperatives. While studying for her MA in Women's Studies at York she became involved with Raw Nerve Books and is a co-director. She now lives in the nuclear-free zone of Takoma Park, Maryland and works as a graphic designer.

Mary Eagleton is reader in the School of Cultural Studies at Leeds Metropolitan University. Her research interests cover contemporary women's fiction and feminist literary theory. Her published works include *Feminist Literary Criticism* (Longman 1991), *Feminist Literary Theory: A Reader* (Blackwell 1996), *Working with Feminist Criticism* (Blackwell 1996), *A Concise Companion to Feminist Theory* (Blackwell 2003). She is at present working on a book for Palgrave on fictional representations of the woman author.

Sarah Edwards completed her MA and PhD at the University of York and is now Lecturer in English Studies at the University of Strathclyde. She has published several articles on *The Country Diary of an Edwardian Lady* and women's life-writing.

Novelist **Zoë Fairbairns** was a founder-member of St Andrews women's liberation group in 1970, information officer at the Women's Research and Resources Centre in London between 1975 and 1977 and poetry editor of *Spare Rib* between 1978 and 1982. Her books include *Benefits*, a feminist dystopia first published in 1979, and most recently, *Other Names*.

Until 1985 **Judy Giles** was a part time secretary, barmaid and dinner lady, bringing up three children. After gaining her first degree she came to the Centre for Women's Studies in York where she completed her doctorate in 1989. Since then she has worked at York St John College teaching and researching women's studies and cultural history.

Helen Graham is currently completing a PhD at the Centre for Women's Studies, University of York on the pitfalls and possibilities bound up in remembering the British Women's Liberation Movement. Although born in 1977 the 'myth' of the radical 'sixties' and 'seventies' looms large in her politics, making her feel by turns resentful, nostalgic, wishful and wanting to forget.

Clare Hemmings is Lecturer in Gender Studies and Gender Theory at the Gender Institute, London School of Economics. She is the author of *Bisexual Spaces: A Geography of Sexuality and Gender* (Routledge 2002), and has published widely within queer and feminist studies over the last 10 years. Her current work is on the narration of the recent feminist past.

Myrtle Hill is a Senior Lecturer and Director of the Centre for Women's Studies at Queen's University Belfast. Her books include *Women of Ireland, Image and Experience c1880-1920* (2nd edtn; Belfast 1999: with Vivienne Pollack). *Women in Ireland 1900-2000*, will be published in September 2003 by Blackstaff Press.

Ann Kaloski works at the Centre for Women's Studies, University of York. Her teaching and research interests revolve around contemporary culture and fiction. She is co-director of Raw Nerve Books and instigator of Wired Women's Studies. <www.annkaloski.net>

Stevi Jackson is Professor of Women's Studies and Director of the Centre for Women's Studies at the University of York. She is the author of *Childhood and Sexuality* (1982), *Christine Delphy* (1996) and *Heterosexuality in Question* (1999). She has co-edited, with Sue Scott, *Feminism and Sexuality* (1996) and *Gender: A Sociological Reader* (2002).

Mary Joannou is Senior Lecturer in English and Women's Studies at Anglia Polytechnic University in Cambridge. She is the author of *Ladies, Please Don't Smash These Windows: Women's Writing, Feminism and Social Change 1918-1938* and *Contemporary Women's Writing: From the Golden Notebook to The Color Purple* and the editor of *Women Writers of the 1930s: Gender, Politics and History*.

Margaretta Jolly teaches in the School of English at the University of Exeter. She is the editor of *The Encyclopedia of Life Writing* (Fitzroy Dearborn 2001) and *Dear Laughing Motorbyke: Letters from Women Welders of the Second World War* (Scarlet Press 1997). She is currently writing a book on the art of letter writing in the women's movement since 1970.

Esperanza Miyake is currently a PhD student at Lancaster University, researching the embodiment of lesbian desire through music.

Ali Neilson is studying for her PhD at the Centre for Women's Studies, University of York. Although still wrinkle-free at twenty-five, her research focuses upon discourses of ageing within contemporary culture, fiction and theory.

Julie Palmer recently completed the MA in Women's Studies at the University of York. She currently works as a research assistant for the University of Wolverhampton, School of Health.

Emma Robertson is a PhD student at the University of York, researching the lives of women workers in the chocolate industry in both York and Nigeria. She completed her MA at the Centre for Women's Studies, where she developed a keen interest in women's history. She is currently working on a web site based on the oral histories of women workers at the local Rowntree factory. <www.cocoareworks.co.uk>

Avril Rolph began research into the Women's Liberation Movement in Wales after moving to South Wales in 1996, after decades of living and working (as a librarian) in London. A committed feminist since the 1970s, Avril is a founder member of Archif Menywod Cymru/Women's Archive of Wales, which rescues and publicises the (badly overlooked) history of women's lives in Wales.

Sue Scott is Professor of Sociology and Postgraduate Dean at the University of Durham. She is currently working with Lydia Martens and Matt Watson on a study of gender and generation in relation to 'everyday kitchen practices'. With Stevi Jackson she has jointly edited the readers *Feminism and Sexuality* (1996) and *Gender* (2002), and they are planning a book on *Theorising Gender and Sexuality*.

In 2000 **Eve Setch** completed a PhD on the history of the Women's Liberation Movement in the 1970s and is currently teaching at the London Metropolitan University.

Sue Thomas's books include the novels *Correspondence* and *Water*, and the story anthology *Wild Women*. An excerpt from *Correspondence* appeared in *Reload: Rethinking Women and Cyberculture*. With Teri Hoskin, she co-edited the *Noon Quilt* website and book. She is Artistic Director of the trAce Online Writing Centre in Nottingham Trent University. <http://trace.ntu.ac.uk/suethomas/>

Imelda Whelehan is Professor of English and Women's Studies at De Montfort University, Leicester. Her publications include *Modern Feminist Thought* (1995) and *Overloaded* (2000). She is currently working on a book about the legacy of the consciousness raising novel.

Other associated publications from Raw Nerve Books

Web Book: *The Feminist Seventies* (June, 2003) is a companion publication edited by the same group of women who produced this print book and is freely available online. <www.feminist-seventies.net/webbook.html>

Pamphlet: Zoë Fairbairns, Helen Graham, Ali Neilson, Emma Robertson, Ann Kaloski (2002). *Saying What We Want: Women's demands in the feminist seventies and now* and its related, interactive web site, *Women Demand.* <www.feminist-seventies.net/womendemand.html>

The Feminist Seventies web site offers links to the web book, to Women Demand, and to the conference archives: <www.feminist-seventies.net>

Full details of these and other Raw Nerve publications available on <www.rawnervebooks.co.uk>

Index

195